30 DAYS TO THE GRE® CAT

4th edition

Rajiv N. Rimal
Peter Z. Orton

THOMSON
™
ARCO

Australia • Canada • Mexico • Singapore • Spain • United Kingdom • United States

An ARCO Book

ARCO is a registered trademark of Thomson Learning, Inc. and is used herein under license by Peterson's.

About The Thomson Corporation and Peterson's

With revenues of US$7.8 billion, The Thomson Corporation (www.thomson.com) is a leading global provider of integrated information solutions for business, education, and professional customers. Its Learning businesses and brands (www.thomsonlearning.com) serve the needs of individuals, learning institutions, and corporations with products and services for both traditional and distributed learning.

Peterson's, part of The Thomson Corporation, is one of the nation's most respected providers of lifelong learning online resources, software, reference guides, and books. The Education Supersite[SM] at www.petersons.com—the Internet's most heavily traveled education resource—has searchable databases and interactive tools for contacting U.S.-accredited institutions and programs. In addition, Peterson's serves more than 105 million education consumers annually.

For more information, contact Peterson's, 2000 Lenox Drive, Lawrenceville, NJ 08648; 800-338-3282; or find us on the World Wide Web at: www.petersons.com/about

ISBN: 0-7689-1343-8

Printed in Canada

10 9 8 7 6 5 4 3 2   05 04

Fourth Edition

Introduction

If you can identify with the two assumptions below, this book is for you.

- Most students postpone preparing for the GRE as long as possible.
- Most students, knowing that their future depends on which ovals they shade and which ones they leave blank, are nervous about taking the GRE.

The authors of *30 Days to the GRE CAT* have written numerous books about standardized tests and taught GRE preparation for many years. They know that your score on the GRE is only one of many components for admission to a graduate program. But they also know that you have to do well on the GRE in order to get into the graduate program of your choice. This book has been prepared with the aim of helping you to:

- Become a great test-taker
- Develop strategies to boost your confidence
- Understand that your performance depends on your familiarity with the test
- Master test-taking skills in a relatively short period of time

Doing well on the GRE requires practice as well as knowledge. This book introduces you to concepts, formulas, and strategies. It also provides full-length practice tests. If you set aside 60 minutes each day to follow this 30-day program, you can substantially improve your score.

Here's what you will find in this book:

- Overall test-taking strategies
- Tips for taking the test on the computer
- Specific strategies for each section of the GRE
- Analysis of answers to test questions
- Full coverage of the Analytical Writing Assessment

Let's be honest. The GRE, for most students, is difficult. We acknowledge that. Based on our experience, however, hard work pays off in higher GRE scores. This book, by itself, won't get you a perfect score. But if you follow our strategies, take the practice tests, review your answers, and learn from your mistakes, you can substantially improve your score. Good luck.

THE 30-DAY PROGRAM

Note: For a more thorough review, math and verbal sections of the test are presented in two parts, labeled (1) and (2). We've also added more questions than will appear on the actual GRE.

Rajiv N
teach
an

About the Authors

Rimal, Ph.D., and Peter Z. Orton, Ph.D., have a combined twenty years' experience ng SAT preparation programs for the California State Universities. Together they wrote d produced "TEAM SAT," a multimedia, interactive CD-ROM program (Zelos Digital earning), which was awarded the "Best of Show" prize at the International Interactive Computer Society's 1995 Summit Awards and the Gold Prize in Interactive Education at the 1995 CINDY Awards.

Dr. Rimal is an Assistant Professor in the Department of Communication Studies at the University of Texas at Austin, where he writes, teaches, and conducts research on human learning.

Dr. Orton is Program Director of Global Learning Technology for IBM Management Development and co-author of fourteen test-preparation textbooks.

Day 1 to **Day 8**

**Test Structure
and Strategies**

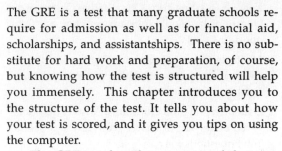

Day 1

Get to Know the GRE

Assignments for Today:

1. Learn the structure of the GRE.
2. Learn how the GRE is scored.
3. Call the schools to which you want to apply.
4. Learn about the computerized version of the GRE.

The GRE is a test that many graduate schools require for admission as well as for financial aid, scholarships, and assistantships. There is no substitute for hard work and preparation, of course, but knowing how the test is structured will help you immensely. This chapter introduces you to the structure of the test. It tells you about how your test is scored, and it gives you tips on using the computer.

The GRE can be taken year-round, but you should register early so that you get your preferred date. There is no deadline to register, but availability is determined by the number of seats available at your testing site. Testing sites run on a first-come, first-served basis. November, December, and January are the busiest months. If you plan to take the GRE during these months, register early. You can take the test only once in any calendar month, and you can take the test up to 5 times in any twelve-month period. This applies even if you canceled your scores on tests taken previously.

At the time of writing this book, the fee structure was as follows:

Test Location	Cost for the GRE
U.S., U.S. Territories, & Puerto Rico	$115
All other locations	$140
Rescheduling fee	$ 40

You can call 1-800-GRE-CALL to find the current cost. You can also find information on line at www.gre.org.

SECTIONS OF THE TEST

The GRE consists of three sections—verbal ability, math ability, and writing ability. Each section is scored separately. Verbal and math sections are each scored from 200 to 800. The writing section consists of two parts: an analysis of an issue essay and an analysis of an argument essay. Each part is scored from 0 to 6, with 6 being the highest, and the final score for the writing section will be the average of the scores from these two sections.

The following chart shows the structure of the test.

A TYPICAL GRE TEST

Section	Time	Questions
Mandatory Tutorial	Variable	Tutorial on using the mouse, selecting an answer, using the testing tools, and scrolling
Verbal Ability	30 minutes	6 sentence completion questions
	30 questions	7 analogy questions
		8 reading comprehension questions
		9 antonym questions
Math Ability	45 minutes	14 quantitative comparison questions
	28 questions	10 five-answer multiple-choice questions
		4 data interpretation questions
Writing Assessment	45 minutes 30 minutes	Issue analysis Argument analysis

Note: On the actual test, these sections may appear in any order.

Mandatory Tutorial

This section gives you a tutorial on using the computer to take the GRE. Even though you may know how to use the mouse, scroll, etc., you will still have to go through the tutorial.

Verbal Ability

The four types of verbal questions are:
1. **Sentence Completion Questions:** Read a sentence that has one or more blanks, and choose the word or words that fit the meaning of the sentence. Total questions = 6
2. **Analogy Questions:** Figure out the relationship between two words, and select the choice that has the same relationship. Total questions = 7
3. **Reading Comprehension Questions:** Read a passage and answer questions based on the passage. Total questions = 8
4. **Antonym Questions:** Find the word most opposite in meaning to the given word. Total questions = 9

Math Ability

The three types of quantitative ability questions are:
1. **Quantitative Comparison Questions:** Compare two quantities and determine which is greater, if they are equal, or if there's no way to determine the relationship. Quantitative Comparison Questions have only four answer choices. Total questions = 14
2. **Multiple-Choice Questions:** Standard multiple-choice math questions, with five answer choices. Total questions = 10
3. **Data Interpretation Questions:** Answer questions based on a chart or charts given in the problem. Total questions = 4

Writing Assessment

The Optional Writing Assessment consists of two parts: the position paper and the argument analysis.
1. **Position Paper:** You will be given two topics and asked to state your position for or against the given topic.
2. **Argument Analysis:** You will be given an argument and asked to analyze it.

SCORING OF THE GRE

You will get three separate scores, one for verbal, one for math, and one for the writing assessment. The verbal and math sections are each scored from 200 (no questions answered correctly) to 800 (all, or nearly all, questions answered correctly). The "median" score is 500, meaning that about half the students taking the test will score higher than 500, and half will score lower than 500. The writing assessment is scored from 0 (poor) to 6 (best).

For the verbal and math sections, you'll know your score immediately after you finish the test. Official scores for all three portions will be mailed to you ten to fifteen days after you take the test—unless you opted to handwrite (instead of typing on the computer) your writing assessment, in which case all three scores will be mailed six weeks after you take the test.

CALL YOUR SCHOOLS

You probably have a number of schools to which you want to apply. Call them today and find out how much you need to score on the GRE to be admitted or to qualify for fellowships. Schools can often give you the average GRE scores of their incoming students. You can use this information to set your own personal GRE goals.

USING THE COMPUTER TO TAKE THE GRE

The GRE is also called the "Computer-Adaptive Test," which means that the computer assesses your ability throughout the test, controls the difficulty level of the questions given to you, and assigns you a score. Here's how the process works.

The first few questions you see will be of medium difficulty level. The computer first asks you questions that about half the test-taking population is likely to answer correctly. If you answer these questions correctly, the computer then begins to increase the difficulty level of the questions given to you. As

you answer more and more questions correctly, the questions get tougher and tougher until either you answer all the questions correctly (in which case, you're likely to get a perfect score) or you answer incorrectly. As soon as you provide an incorrect answer, the difficulty level of the subsequent question drops. If you answer the first few questions incorrectly, the computer decreases the difficulty level of the questions and hence sets a ceiling for your score. In other words, your score on the GRE depends not only on the number of questions you answer correctly, but also on the difficulty level of those questions.

This idea that the computer is constantly monitoring your ability makes a lot of people nervous. What this means to you, however, is that you should pay close attention to the first few questions. Take a little more time if you have to. Don't let the computer set the ceiling for your score early on in the test.

The computer also "demands" that you provide an answer for each question. You won't be able to skip. Hence, if you find yourself stuck, take an educated guess (strategies in this book will help you do this).

Elements of the Computer Screen

The questions that appear on the computer screen on the GRE will look different than a paper-based test. Notice that the answer choices won't be labeled (A), (B), (C), (D), and (E). Instead, there are ovals that you click on to register an answer. The different elements of the screen are:

Time

The screen shows the amount of time remaining for the section that you are working on. If you want, you can choose to hide this clock. However, toward the end of the section, this clock will automatically reappear to warn you about the time remaining.

Question Number

This tells you what question you are currently working on and the total number of questions for the section. For example, a "5 of 30" on the screen means that you are on the fifth question out of 30 in the section.

Test Quit

You can choose to quit to stop the test at any time. If you choose this option, you won't know your score. Use this option only if something drastic happens.

Section Exit

You can skip the remaining questions in the section by choosing this option.

Help

Press this button if you need help.

Next

After you fill in the oval to indicate your answer, press this button. The "Answer Confirm" button will then light up. This is the computer's way of asking you, "Is this your final answer?" You can choose another answer at this point if you change your mind. Otherwise, if you confirm your answer, you will be taken to the next screen.

Finally, before you take the test, make sure that you brush up on your typing skills. You will be at a disadvantage if you are not able to type efficiently.

Day 2

General Strategies

Assignment for Today:

Learn seven important test-taking strategies.

TEST STRATEGY 1.
Pay Special Attention to the First Few Questions

On the GRE, the first few questions are immensely important. They will be used to set the ceiling for your score. If you answer these questions correctly, the subsequent questions get tougher, which means that your score will get better. If you answer the first few questions incorrectly, the questions get easier, which means that your score will become lower. Hence, it is important that you answer these questions with care. Take some extra time if you have to. Check your answer before you confirm your final answer.

TEST STRATEGY 2.
Eliminate the Losers

Do you know what the directions on your test say? They ask you to choose not the right answer, but the best answer. Why "best"? Because the "right" answer may not even be in the choices. So sometimes you've got to settle for the best of what they offer, and the best may not be great.

Suppose you read a passage, and it's all about how to improve your social life in college. One question might go something like this:

Which of the following is the most appropriate title for this passage?

Now you're thinking the title ought to be something like "How to improve a college social life," "How college students can improve their social life," "How a college social life can be improved," or some arrangement of those words.

But on the GRE, there's a good chance that none of these will be among the choices.

Let's look at the choices:

(A) Improving your high school social life

(B) Improving your social life in school

(C) Improving your test scores in college

(D) Improving quality of life in college

(E) How to publish in graduate school

Before you answer questions like this one, we strongly recommend the following strategy: On your scratch paper, write:

A   B   C   D   E

Then, as you spot incorrect choices, cross them out — yes, literally cross them out with your pencil.

Choice (A) has two key words wrong: high school. The passage was about the social life of college students, so the words "high school" make this choice off-topic and wrong. At this point, take your pencil and cross out choice (A) so that your scratch paper now looks like:

~~A~~   B   C   D   E

Now to choice (B). This says, "Improving your social life in school." For it to be perfect, it should read "Improving your social life in college." Just the word "school," by itself, is too general. But so far, it's better than choice (A), and it might be the best answer of all. So quickly draw a question mark and keep going. So now, your scratch paper should look like this:

~~A~~   ?B   C   D   E

Choice (C) is highly commendable but off topic. Cross out choice (C) so that you now have:

~~A~~   ?B   ~~C~~   D   E

Choice (D), "Improving the quality of life in college" is also not perfect. You'd like it to read "Improving the quality of social life in college." Here you have "college," but you don't have "social" life. So what do you do? It's too general, but it's possible, so consider it. Put a question mark beside it. So now you have:

~~A~~   ?B   ~~C~~   ?D   E

Choice (E) would certainly improve your college academic life, but it's off topic. Eliminate choice (E) so that you now have:

~~A~~   ?B   ~~C~~   ?D   ~~E~~

So now you're down to two possible answers.

Compare choice (B) against choice (D) to find the better one, but even if you can't find the one winner, you've narrowed five choices down to just two, so take your best guess and move on.

Eliminating wrong choices not only saves time but also helps you get more questions right. So remember, eliminate the losers and come out a winner.

TEST STRATEGY 3.
Guess Smart

On the computer-adaptive test, you cannot leave any questions blank; you have to answer each question before the computer allows you to move on to the next one. So what do you do if you get stuck? Take an educated guess. Before you take a random guess, see if you can knock out one or two answer choices. That way, you can improve your odds. Look at this example from an antonym section (in which you have to find the word that means opposite of the given word):

BELLIGERENT:

- aggressive
- hostile
- uplift
- painful
- amiable

Suppose you had no idea what belligerent meant. One way to take a guess would be to get a feel for the word. If even this strategy doesn't work, think about other words that have the same prefix (e.g., bellicose, which means hostile). You'll find that words with "belli" as the prefix usually mean something negative. If you got this far, you would see that "aggressive," "hostile," and "painful" are all negative, which means that they cannot be the correct answer because we're looking for the opposite of belligerent. The only two words that are positive are "uplift" and "amiable." Here's another important clue: The part of speech of the main word (belligerent, which is an adjective) will always be the same as the part of speech of the correct answer. Notice that "uplift" is a verb ("uplifting" would be an adjective), and so you can knock this out. You're now left with only one answer, the correct one, amiable.

So, if you have to guess, pause for a second to see if you can come up with some strategy that will allow you to knock out one or more answer choices.

TEST STRATEGY 4.
Answer What's Asked

One way people lose points on the GRE is that they know how to work a problem, but they don't read the question correctly. This should never happen to you. Take a look at this question.

If $3n - 7 = 2$, what is $5n$?

(A) 3

(B) 6

(C) 9

(D) 12

(E) 15

You might answer this question this way:

$$3n = 2 + 7$$
$$3n = 9$$
$$n = \frac{9}{3}$$
$$n = 3$$

At this point, you might think choice (A) is your answer, because n equals 3. But the answer is NOT 3 because the question asks for the value of $5n$, not n. You have to take the value of n (3) and multiply by 5 to get choice (E), 15.

This might look simple enough, but imagine you're taking your test. You're under time pressure, you've been working for several hours under severe stress, your concentration's starting to flag, and the person sitting behind you is tapping his pencil and sniffling.

Under such conditions, it's easy to misread the question and answer the wrong thing. So what can you do?

Here's something that can help.

As you read a problem, identify what you finally have to solve for, and write it down! Writing it down helps you focus on your final goal. And it helps you avoid the common misreading errors built into the test.

You should also use this strategy on the reading questions of your test. What would you write down in this typical reading question: "With which of the following would the author disagree?"

"Disagree" or "author disagree" is really the heart of the question. You're looking for an answer that's *opposite* to the author's point of view. If you write "author disagree," you will avoid misreading the question.

Writing your "goal" is a super strategy to make sure you answer what's asked. The worst thing to happen on your test is to know how to work a problem, spend time working it, and yet get it wrong because you answered the wrong thing. Writing your "goal" helps you get those questions right.

TEST STRATEGY 5.
Get Lots of Scratch Paper

From the previous strategy, you may have noticed that you will be using a lot of scratch paper. Get lots of it before you sit down at your computer. You don't want to be wasting valuable test time walking over to the test administrator to ask for more paper. There is no limit on how much paper you can use. At the end of the test, you'll be required to turn everything in anyway, so there's no penalty for taking lots of paper with you. If you don't use it, just return it.

TEST STRATEGY 6.
Don't Read the Directions

Here's a quick tip that will save you time, and because it saves you time, it will help you get a few more questions right: Do not waste time reading directions on your test. The more time you spend reading the directions, the less time you have to answer questions. So what should you do? Work through this program. By the time you finish, you'll know the directions for every question type inside and out. And you'll also know which strategies and tips to use for which questions.

Here's a quick list of question types for your review:

Verbal Section

1. Reading comprehension—Read the passage and answer questions based on what's stated or implied in the passage.
2. Sentence completion—Select the word or words that best complete the sentence from the list of choices.
3. Analogies—Find the relationship between the two words in the question and look for the answer choice that has the same relationship.
4. Antonyms—Find the word that is most opposite in meaning to the given word.

Math Section

1. Problem solving—Solve the problem and find the answer from among the five choices given.
2. Quantitative comparison—Compare the two columns and choose:

   (A) if Column A is greater than Column B,

   (B) if Column B is greater than Column A,

   (C) if Column A is equal to Column B, or

   (D) if the relationship cannot be determined based on the information given.

   Do not select choice (E). There is no such choice in this question type.
3. Data interpretation—Answer questions based on one or more charts given in the problem.

Writing Assessment

1. **Position Paper:** Choose one of two given topics and state your position for or against the topic. (45 minutes)
2. **Argument Analysis**: Analyze the given argument. (30 minutes)

Instant Replay: Test Strategies

1. Pay special attention to the first few questions.

2. Eliminate the losers.

3. Guess smart.

4. Answer what's asked.

5. Get lots of scratch paper.

6. Don't read the directions.

Day 3

Verbal Strategies: Reading and Analogies

Assignments for Today:

1. Learn reading comprehension strategies and question types.
2. Learn analogy strategies and question types.

READING COMPREHENSION QUESTIONS

The reading part of the verbal section provides you with a passage and asks you to answer a number of questions based on the content of the passage. Here are some useful strategies for this section.

READING STRATEGY 1.
No Need to Read the Questions First

A frequently asked question is: "Should I read the questions first?" While the advantage of reading the questions first, before you read the passage, is that you will get a general feel for the kinds of questions for which you'll need to read the passage, our experience is that this technique wastes a lot of time. On the test, it is quite likely that you will forget the content of the questions as you begin reading the passage. So we suggest that you dive into the passage right away and not waste any time.

READING STRATEGY 2.
Use Only What You Read

The reading questions test only what's *in* the passage, so don't bring in any outside information. Use only what's stated or implied in the passage, even if you know a lot about the topic.

READING STRATEGY 3.
Let the Paragraphs Help

A reading passage can seem really long. But the author has already broken it down for you into manageable pieces—the paragraphs. Don't try to rush through from the first word to the last word. That's not the best way to read. Instead, read paragraph by paragraph. After reading the first paragraph, take a quick mental breath and think to yourself, "What, briefly, was that paragraph about?" Then read the next paragraph and do that again. And then do the same for the one after that. When you finish the passage, what have you done? You've summarized all the important ideas in the passage.

READING STRATEGY 4.
Read Actively

As you read the passage, you should take notes on a piece of paper. Most people cannot remember the content of the paragraph without taking notes. If you come across an important idea, write down the key words and phrases. Draw arrows from one word to another. Mark plus (supporting idea) and minus (refuting idea) next to words and phrases. Put a line through words if the author disagrees with the idea represented in the phrase. Here's an example:

Passage on the screen:

Genetically altered crops are supposed to ameliorate hunger-related problems throughout the world. It is said that, by altering the genetic composition of rice, wheat, soybeans, and other crops, their yield will substantially increase. Hence, as the global population increases, amount of land devoted to agriculture will not have to increase in the same proportion. The problem is that many people are hesitant to consume genetically altered food. If recent trend is any indication, more and more people are demanding to know which food on the supermarket shelf has been genetically altered and then they are staying clear of those foods. So, while yield may increase substantially, demand for the genetically altered crops is likely to wane considerably.

Notes you could take:

FOR	AGAINST
GAC —> hunger reduction	Hesitant consumers
GAC —> greater yield	Want information
—>less land for farming	—>stay clear

READING STRATEGY 5.
Make a Movie in Your Head

What if you're reading a passage and nothing is sinking in? The clock's ticking, and you have no idea of what you just read. This happens to all of us. If it happens to you, the best thing to do is to "make a movie" in your head. Believe it or not, you understand better if you visualize what you read. Don't memorize, just visualize. As you read the passage, form interesting pictures in your head.

READING STRATEGY 6.
Know the Different Types
of Reading Questions

Here are the most common types of reading questions. Familiarize yourself with these question types so that when you see them on the test, you'll know what they are asking you to do.

Type 1: Main Idea

For each passage, you'll be asked to determine the main idea. Sometimes the question says just that: "What is the main idea of the passage?" Or it can use other words, such as, "What is the most appropriate title of the passage?" or, "What is the author's central argument?" or, "The passage is primarily concerned with the subject of . . ." Each of these questions asks the same thing: What is the main theme of the passage? The correct answer to a "main idea" question isn't necessarily found in the first sentence or the last. These may, or may not, express the "main idea." But the main idea is *always* a theme that runs through most, if not all, of the paragraphs.

Type 2: Vocabulary

Some questions ask you to define words or phrases from the passage. To do this, you'll have to look back to where the word or phrase was used and see what it means as it's used in that particular sentence. For example, the question might say, "The word 'estate' in line 46 most nearly means . . ." Depending on the sentence, "estate" could mean someone's property, someone's status, a piece of land, or even an inheritance. To figure out which sense is meant, start from a little before line 46, and read through that line and past it. You'll then have a handle on what the author meant by that term. Then answer the question.

Type 3: Specific Information

Some questions ask about specific information from the passage. For example, the question might say, "The passage mentions which of the following as important to the success of a feature film?" or, "The author discusses the hobbies of which Presidents?" or, "The incident in lines 21–35 describes which of the following?" If you can answer these from what you remember having read in the passage, great! Otherwise, simply go back to the paragraph, find that part, and reread enough to find the answer.

Type 4: Author's Point-of-View

Another type of question asks you to determine the author's tone or point of view. For example, the question might say, "The author's attitude toward large dogs is . . .," or, "The author believes strongly that . . .," or, "The author would most likely agree with which of the following?" As you read, small details should help you become aware of how the author of the passage feels about the topic presented. Is the author in favor . . . or opposed . . . or neutral . . . or sarcastic . . . or doubtful . . . or excited?

Type 5: Reasoning

And finally, questions also ask you to apply or interpret what you just read. For example, the question might say, "The author most likely describes the traffic on the highway in order to . . . ," or, "The reference to loud chewing is inappropriate as an argument for gum control because . . . ," or, "The description of George Washington's cow serves to . . . ." Reasoning questions are usually the toughest because the answers won't be stated directly in the passage. You have to read beneath the surface. But you still can't bring in your own information. You can use only what the author implies.

ANALOGY QUESTIONS

Another of the verbal question types on your test is analogies. Analogies look like this:

STEM:WORDS::

- **(A)** first pair
- **(B)** second pair
- **(C)** third pair
- **(D)** fourth pair
- **(E)** fifth pair

ANALOGY STRATEGY 1.
Figure Out the Relationship
Between the Stem Words

The analogy questions on your test follow a simple rule. First you find the relationship between the stem words, and then you find that same relationship in one of the choices. Let's try one.

SKYSCRAPER:SHACK::
- **(A)** elevator:escalator
- **(B)** house:building
- **(C)** village:town
- **(D)** jetliner:biplane
- **(E)** chimney:fireplace

The stem words are *skyscraper* and *shack*. What's the relationship between skyscraper and shack? A skyscraper is a large, modern structure. A shack is a small structure. So the relationship is: the first word is a large, modern version of the second word.

ANALOGY STRATEGY 2.
Find the Same Relationship Between the
Words in One of the Answer Choices

Once you know how the stem words are related, your next job is to find the one answer choice that best matches this relationship. Let's try the answer choices above one at a time.

Choice (A): Is the first word, *elevator*, a large, modern version of the second word, *escalator*? Obviously not. So knock this choice out.

Choice (B): Is a *house* a large, modern version of a *building*? Not at all. So cross out this choice.

Choice (C): Is a *village* a large, modern version of a *town*? Of course not. So eliminate this choice.

Choice (D): Is a *jetliner* a large, modern version of a *biplane*? Yes. A jetliner is a large, modern aircraft. A biplane is one of those small double-wing planes with two seats. So the relationship in this choice matches the relationship of the stem words. The first word is a large, modern version of the second word. Looks like you have a winner. Mark it, but let's look at the remaining choice, just in case.

Choice (E): Is a *chimney* a large, modern version of a *fireplace*? Well, a chimney is a part of a fireplace, not a modern version of it. Even though this choice has something to do with buildings, its relationship doesn't match, so knock it out.

Did you notice something? The stem words are about buildings, but the correct answer has nothing to do with buildings. You're looking for same relationships, not same categories. The first word was a-modern-and-big "whatever the second word was."

ANALOGY STRATEGY 3.
Consider Starting with the Second Stem Word

Sometimes it's easier to define the relationship between the stem words if you start with the second word in the pair instead of the first one. Let's look at another analogy question to see how this strategy works.

SPORT:SOCCER::

(A) fish:river

(B) volleyball:net

(C) field:fun

(D) stadium:game

(E) literature:sonnet

Here it's easier to say, "Soccer is a kind of sport." The second word is a specific type of the first word. Can you find the choice where the second word is a specific type of the first word?

The correct answer is choice (E). A sonnet is a type of literature. Remember: Whatever order you choose to use in the stem words must be the same order you use in the choices.

ANALOGY STRATEGY 4.
Use the Answer Choices to Determine the Part of Speech of the Stem Words

Sometimes you need to know the part of speech of the stem words in order to determine their meaning and figure out how they are related. For example, suppose you have this question:

SPRING:RAIN::

(A) suitor:gifts

(B) pollen:bee

(C) farm:tractor

(D) automobile:traffic

(E) requirement:limitation

The stem words are puzzling. Is *spring* the action verb meaning *jump* or *bounce*? Or is spring a *thing*, the noun that means the season? Or is it the noun that means the coiled piece of metal that you find in mattresses and watches? One way to find out is to look at the answer choices. Are the first words in the answer choices verbs or nouns?

Farm can be either a verb or a noun, but the other first words are nouns. So from that you know that all the first words are nouns, including *spring* and *farm*. We don't know what the second words are yet. But now that you know the stem word *spring* is a noun—not the verb that means to jump—can you find the answer to this question?

Choice (A) is the right answer. Spring, the season, brings rain, in the same way that a suitor brings gifts.

Questions like that one can be tricky if a word has more than one meaning. If you try one meaning and have no luck, try another meaning and see if that one works. But once you know a word is, say, a noun, try only different noun meanings, not meanings of verbs or adjectives.

ANALOGY STRATEGY 5.
Make Sure You Know the Most Common Analogy Relationships

Here are the 11 most common GRE analogy relationships:

1. Type of.

SOCCER:SPORT:: You saw one like this before, remember? Soccer is a type of sport. Here's another example: JAYWALK:MISDEMEANOR:: Jaywalk is a type of misdemeanor, or minor crime.

2. Definition.

PROCRASTINATOR:DELAY:: A procrastinator is someone who delays. Or you could say that delay is what a procrastinator does. Whatever order you use for the stem words is the order you must use for each of the choices.

3. Opposites.

STARVATION:BINGING:: Starvation is the opposite of binging.

4. Lack of.

PAUPER:MONEY:: A pauper lacks money. The first word lacks the second word.

5. Same.

PERSUASIVE:CONVINCING:: Someone who is persuasive is also convincing; the two words are synonyms.

6. Extremes.

HOT:SCALDING:: The second word is the extreme of the first word.

7. Part-to-whole.

PLATOON:SOLDIER:: The second word is part of the first word.

8. Use.

GILLS:BREATHING:: Gills are used for breathing. The first word is used for the purpose of the second word.

9. Place.

DESERT:OASIS:: The second word is located in the first word.

10. Sign of.

SNARL:ANGER:: The first word is a sign of the second word.

11. Job-related pairs.

Analogies that have to do with jobs or work also appear on your test. For example:

   a)   SURGERY:INCISION:: An incision is performed in surgery. The second word is something that is done during the first word.

   b)   SCALPEL:SURGERY:: A scalpel—which is a doctor's cutting tool—is used in surgery. The first word is a tool used for doing the second word.

   c)   CONSTRUCTION:CARPENTER:: The second word is someone who performs the first word.

ANALOGY STRATEGY 6.
Practice With Lots of Analogy Questions

The best thing you can do to improve your analogy score is to practice answering analogy questions. That way, you can learn the many types of analogies, practice using the strategies, and learn meanings of new words. There are many analogy questions in this book. Make sure you do them all.

Instant Replay: Reading and Analogies

Reading

1. No need to read the questions first.

2. Use only what you read.

3. Let the paragraphs help.

4. Read actively.

5. Make a movie in your head.

6. Know the different types of reading questions.

Analogies

1. Figure out the relationship between the stem words.

2. Find the same relationship between the words in one of the answer choices.

3. Consider starting with the second stem word.

4. Use the answer choices to determine the part of speech of the stem words.

5. Make sure you know the most common analogy relationships.

6. Practice with lots of analogy questions.

Verbal Strategies: Sentence Completion and Antonyms

Assignments for Today:

1. Learn important sentence completion strategies.
2. Learn important antonym strategies.

SENTENCE COMPLETION QUESTIONS

In this section of your test, all you do is fill in the blanks. But, you've got to find the choice that makes the most sense. Here's an example.

Although my uncle is usually a generous person, yesterday he gave _____ to a woman soliciting for a popular charity.

(A) money

(B) advice

(C) thanks

(D) nothing

(E) food

SENTENCE COMPLETION STRATEGY 1.

Use Your Own Word

What word best fits the blank in the sentence above? The correct answer is choice (D), *nothing*. Although my uncle is usually a generous person, yesterday he gave *nothing* to a woman soliciting for a popular charity.

Were you able to guess what word fit the blank even before looking at the choices? If you could, that was a great way to answer the question. But that's something you can do only on the easiest sentence completion questions. So here's another strategy you can try.

SENTENCE COMPLETION STRATEGY 2.

Look for Flag Words

Certain words—called flag words—give important information about the direction of a sentence. For example, here the flag word is "although," because "although" changed the direction of the sentence. "*Although* my uncle is usually a generous person, yesterday he gave *nothing* . . . " The first part of the sentence describes the guy as generous. But in the second part, he isn't generous at all. The word "although" reversed the direction of the sentence, signaling that the correct completion will be the opposite of *generous*.

Now suppose instead of *although*, the flag word is "since." Now try completing the sentence . . . *Since* my uncle is usually a generous person, yesterday he gave _____ to a woman soliciting for a popular charity. Now the word "money" fits.

The word "since" continues the direction of the sentence. The first part says that uncle is generous, and the second part continues that thought. "*Since* my uncle is usually a generous person, yesterday he gave *money* to a woman soliciting for a popular charity."

So there are two kinds of flags:

- **Opposite flags.** These are words and phrases that reverse the direction of a sentence Opposite flags include: *although, despite, but, even though, instead of, nevertheless, contrary to, rather than, in spite of,* and *however*.

- **Same flags.** These are words that continue the direction of a sentence. Same flags include words like *since, thus, therefore, as, hence, because, for, for instance, and, moreover, so, due to*, and, check this out, a semicolon (;), which also continues the thought of the sentence.

Let's look at this example:

Julia had spent the entire previous week studying; on her final examination, she encountered ____ difficulties.

(A) myriad

(B) frequent

(C) formidable

(D) few

(E) remarkable

This sentence contains a semicolon, which is a same flag. It continues the same feeling or thought throughout the entire sentence. In the first part of the sentence, you learned that Julia spent quite some time studying and so the idea is that she's preparing well for the test. Now continue this thought. She was prepared, so what did she encounter on the test? *Lots* of difficulty? No. Continue the thought: Julia will find almost *no* difficulty on the test. The choice that gives that meaning is "few."

SENTENCE COMPLETION STRATEGY 3.
Try the Second Blank First

Quite a few GRE sentence completion questions have two blanks instead of one. Sometimes the second blank is easier to fill in than the first blank. Look at this example:

Even though he had not eaten all day and had ____ money in his pocket, David ____ the offer of a free meal.

(A) considerable..refused

(B) various..accepted

(C) extra..renegotiated

(D) little..declined

(E) enough..applauded

The flag words "even though" tell you that the direction of the sentence will reverse. The first part of the sentence tells you that David hasn't eaten all day so he must be hungry. The flags "even though" tell you that in the second part of the sentence, David will do the opposite of what his hunger would cause him to do. The two choices that work for the second blank are choice (A), refused, and choice (D), declined. So knock out choices (B), (C), and (E). Now try each of the remaining choices.

First try choice (A). "Even though he had not eaten all day and had considerable money in his pocket, David refused the offer of a free meal." The second blank works fine, but the first word, "considerable," doesn't make much sense. Remember that the flag "even though" tells you that the direction should change. If David had considerable money, he *could* refuse a free meal—nothing surprising about that. There's no change of direction.

So try choice (D). "Even though he had not eaten all day and had little money in his pocket, David declined the offer of a free meal." The second blank works as before, but now the first blank also works. Even though he had little money and was hungry, David said "no" to a free meal. With little money, we would have expected him to jump at the chance for a free meal. But the flag words "even though" told you that the direction of the sentence will reverse and the opposite will happen. And so it did!

SENTENCE COMPLETION STRATEGY 4.
Try All the Choices

In the question above, you had to read only two choices to find the winner. But for some questions, you may have to read all five choices. That happens when there are no flag words, when the sentence is very long, or when it's just plain tough. Here is an example:

> The team members had few, if any, _____ about postponing those long, arduous practice sessions that tended only to deflate their enthusiasm, _____ their coach's frustration at their inconsistent execution.
>
> **(A)** desires..undermining
>
> **(B)** misgivings..increasing
>
> **(C)** hesitations..embracing
>
> **(D)** qualifications..ceasing
>
> **(E)** ideas..reducing

It's hard to tell what's going on. On your test, it may be better to come back to a question like this and do it at the end, since it's probably going to take a lot of time. But when you do come back to it, try reading in each choice to see which makes the most sense.

Let's try choice (A): "The team members had few, if any, *desires* about postponing those long, arduous practice sessions that tended only to deflate their enthusiasm, *undermining* their coach's frustration . . ." Long practice sessions that deflate enthusiasm wouldn't *undermine* (or lessen) their coach's frustration; they would increase it. Forget this choice.

Choice (B): "The team members had few, if any, *misgivings* about postponing those long, arduous practice sessions that tended only to deflate their enthusiasm, *increasing* their coach's frustration at their inconsistent execution." This works. The team had no problem with postponing the dreaded prac-

tices, and these practices not only deflated the team's enthusiasm but also increased their coach's frustration at the team's lousy work. This is a winner, so mark it.

But try the others, just in case one of them is better than choice (B). Choice (C): "The team members had few if any *hesitations* about postponing those long, arduous practice sessions that tended only to deflate their enthusiasm, *embracing* their coach's frustration at their inconsistent execution." "Embracing their coach's frustration" doesn't make much sense in the context of this sentence, and besides, it's not anywhere as good as choice (B). Strike it and keep going.

Choice (D): "The team members had few if any *qualifications* about postponing those long, arduous practice sessions that tended only to deflate their enthusiasm, *ceasing* their coach's frustration at their inconsistent execution." Here, too, the last phrase, "ceasing their coach's frustration," just doesn't make sense in this sentence. Strike this one and check the last one.

Choice (E): "The team members had few if any *ideas* about postponing those long, arduous practice sessions that tended only to deflate their enthusiasm, *reducing* their coach's frustration at their inconsistent execution." This also doesn't make much sense with the entire sentence. The team had no ideas about postponing a practice, and the tough practice reduced the coach's frustration at the team's lousy play? It just doesn't fit right. And certainly it doesn't make the kind of sense that choice (B) does.

Reading in each choice and checking for its meaning is time-consuming. But it's a last-ditch strategy that you'll probably need to use from time to time.

SENTENCE COMPLETION STRATEGY 5.
Read in Your Answer Choice

Even if you don't read all the answer choices into the original sentence, you should at least read in the one you picked as the correct answer. That will help you make sure it fits in the meaning of the sentence.

ANTONYM QUESTIONS

The antonym questions in the verbal section test your vocabulary. You have to know the meaning of a word, and then select the choice that's *opposite* in meaning to that word. Here's an easy example:

ROUGH:

(A) large

(B) round

(C) smooth

(D) reliable

(E) friendly

ANTONYM STRATEGY 1.
Define the Word

The first strategy for attacking antonym questions is to read the stem word (the word in capital letters at the top) and define that word. Do your best to determine its meaning. In this case, you probably have a picture in your mind of "rough" being something that's jagged, bumpy, or bristly.

ANTONYM STRATEGY 2.
Come up with Your Own Opposite Word

Once you have defined the stem word, think of a word that you consider to be its opposite. In the case of *rough*, you might think of the word *smooth* as its opposite. Now look for your word among the answer choices. If it's there, that's great—you've solved the problem. If it's not, your word will give you a clue to the kind of word you're looking for. In the case of *rough*, if *smooth* isn't among the answer choices, you know you're looking for a word like *smooth* that's also an opposite of *rough*. Looking at the answers, one of the choices might be *sleek. Sleek* means the same as *smooth* and is another opposite of *rough*, so it is the correct answer.

If the antonym questions on the GRE were this easy, then these two strategies—define the stem word and then come up with your own opposite—would be all you'd need. Unfortunately, all the questions aren't this easy, which is why you'll need more strategies.

ANTONYM STRATEGY 3.
Put the Word in Context

Sometimes when you're faced with a difficult stem word in an antonym question, you'll realize you've heard the word used before but you can't pin down its exact definition. But if you can place the word in a familiar phrase or sentence, you can help yourself remember what it means and choose the correct answer. For example, consider the following antonym question:

VETO:

(A) refuse

(B) reject

(C) disengage

(D) allow

(E) vote

You've no doubt heard the word *veto* before, but you may have trouble defining it precisely. Do you remember how you heard it used? Perhaps you heard a news report that "the president vetoed the bill." What does that mean? It means that the president cancelled the bill and stopped it from becoming law. Now what's the opposite of *stop*? That's right, *allow*.

What we've just done was to put the stem word "in context."

Whenever you can't immediately pinpoint the stem word's meaning, try putting it in context.

ANTONYM STRATEGY 4.
Identify the Word's Emotional Charge

Sometimes you won't know the exact definition of the stem word of an antonym question, and you won't be able to use it in any particular context. But even if you don't know the word's exact meaning, you may have a good sense of its "emotional charge." What's an emotional charge?

Many words will have either a positive or negative feeling to them. Take this word: *virulent*. How does it sound to you? Positive or negative? *Virulent* means poisonous or deadly. But even if you didn't know its exact meaning, if you felt it sounded negatively charged, you could look for its opposite—a positively charged word—as the correct answer.

Let's look at the choices.

VIRULENT:

(A) deadly

(B) malignant

(C) benign

(D) bacterial

(E) yellow

Choices (A) and (B) are extremely negative. In fact, these are good definitions of the word *virulent*. Since you are looking for an opposite, something positive, eliminate choices (A) and (B). Choice (C) looks possible. *Benign* means gentle or kind. Since it's positive, you should consider it. Choice (D), *bacterial*, sounds like bacteria, which feels negative. Eliminate it. Finally, choice (E) is neutral. Since you're looking for a positive word, eliminate it. Even if you didn't know the meaning of the word *virulent*, you could have used its negative emotional charge to help you select its opposite, a positive word.

ANTONYM STRATEGY 5.
Look for Clues in Word Parts

Word roots, prefixes, and suffixes can offer important clues to help you solve GRE antonym questions. Let's look at an example. Suppose an antonym question looked like this:

MORIBUND:

(A) contentious

(B) malignant

(C) pretentious

(D) detestable

(E) vital

You may not know the meaning of the word *moribund*, but you may know that the word part *mor-* signifies death, as in the word *mortal*. So its opposite would be a word that in some way signifies life or good health. The correct answer is choice (E), *vital*.

Whereas memorizing extensive word lists is probably a waste of time, knowing prefixes, suffixes, and roots can be extremely helpful for this question type.

As you practice the many antonym questions in the test section of this book, pay careful attention to prefixes, suffixes, and roots, and learn them as you work problems. You will probably see them again when you take the real exam.

ANTONYM STRATEGY 6.
Look for Clues in Parts of Speech

Sometimes an antonym question will be difficult because you aren't certain which of the several meanings of the stem word is meant. For example, you might see this question:

FREQUENT:

(A) mean

(B) content

(C) disturb

(D) evade

(E) reserve

Frequent has several meanings, depending on its part of speech. As a verb, *to frequent* means *to visit.* "I used to frequent the casino until I lost all my money." But as an adjective, *frequent* means many or repeated. "The hospital made frequent requests for blood." Which meaning works in this question—the verb or the adjective?

One way to find out is to look at the answer choices. Each antonym question will use only one part of speech. That means that if the stem word is a verb, all the choices in that question are verbs. If the stem word is a noun, all the choices in that question are nouns.

So you can sometimes get a big hint by checking the part of speech of the answer choices. In the question above, choices (A) and (B) can be both verbs and adjectives, so they aren't much help. But choices (C), *disturb*, and (D), *evade*, can be only verbs—so all the choices must therefore be considered as verbs, and the stem word too must be a verb. Now you know that the stem word is the verb *to frequent*, meaning to visit. And you can solve the problem by choosing the opposite of *to frequent*, which is choice (D), *evade*.

So remember, knowing parts of speech can be extremely helpful when you're working antonym questions.

ANTONYM STRATEGY 7.

Consider Alternate Meanings

Difficult analogy questions sometimes use a stem word that has several meanings, all of which are the same part of speech. For instance, try this one:

ORDER:

(A) menu

(B) list

(C) chaos

(D) summons

(E) paper

Notice that choice (A), *menu*, can only be a noun, so the stem word *order* must also be a noun. But even just as a noun, *order* has many meanings. If you think of it as the command, as in "The general gave an order to the troops," you won't find an opposite. So what is another definition for *order*, besides command, that's also a noun?

You might come up with *pattern, organization*, or even *calm*. Now look through the choices. Choice (C), *chaos*, is the opposite of *pattern, organization*, and *calm*. It's the correct choice.

So another important strategy is to remember that many words have multiple meanings and to consider other meanings if your first definition doesn't work.

Instant Replay: Sentence Completions and Antonyms

Sentence Completions

1. Use your own word.

2. Look for flag words.

3. Try the second blank first.

4. Try all the choices.

5. Read in your answer choice.

Antonyms

1. Define the word.

2. Come up with your own opposite word.

3. Put the word in context.

4. Identify the word's emotional charge.

5. Look for clues in word parts.

6. Look for clues in parts of speech.

7. Consider alternate meanings.

Math Strategies: Problem Solving

Assignment for Today:

Learn problem-solving strategies for multiple-choice math problems.

MATH STRATEGY 1.

Scan the Choices

The answer choices on the GRE tell us a lot about how to solve the problem. Many people are surprised when they find out that the answer choices give away a lot of information. Here's an example.

What is the sum of the lowest factors of 8 and 6?

(A) −48

(B) −14

(C) 2

(D) 10

(E) 24

Can you think of the answer? Before you find out whether you got the right answer, think about this important rule: Always scan the answers before you work on a problem.

Did you think about your answers again? You have probably guessed by now that the correct answer is not choice (C), 2. If you scanned the answers before you solved this question, you may have seen that two of the answer choices were negative numbers. This should give you an important clue.

Yes, −6 is also a factor of 6 because −6 × −1 = 6 and −8 is a factor of 8 because −8 × −1 = 8. And so the correct answer is choice (B), −14.

Quite often, when you're asked to find the area or the circumference of a circle, you'll notice that the answer choices all have a π in them. This immediately tells you that you don't need to convert π to 3.14. You can leave π as π and work the problem.

So, remember this important strategy. Always scan the answers before you start a problem.

MATH STRATEGY 2.
See How It Ends

Here's a dandy shortcut to use when you multiply numbers. Suppose you were asked to multiply 356 and 39 and were given the following choices:

(A) 13,781

(B) 13,723

(C) 13,884

(D) 14,875

(E) 15,233

You should be able to tell that the right answer is choice (C). How? It's easy if you just "see how it ends." To see how this works, let's take a problem that's more like the ones you'll find on the GRE:

Tickets to a concert cost $36 each. What is the total cost of each ticket if there is a 6% sales tax?

(A) $ 2.16

(B) $36.00

(C) $36.22

(D) $38.16

(E) $39.24

The first thing you should realize is that because of the sales tax, the total cost will be more than $36. At this point, you can knock out choices (A) and (B) because they are not more than $36.

One way to solve this problem is to find 6% of $36 and add that amount to $36. Another way is to find 106% of $36, and you would do that by multiplying 1.06 by 36.

$$\begin{array}{r} 1.06 \\ \times\, 36 \\ \hline \end{array}$$

What happens when you multiply the two 6's together? Your answer will end in a 6 because $6 \times 6 = 36$. In other words, the correct answer should be greater than $36 and it should end in a 6. Now look at your answer choices. Which answer choice is greater than $36 and ends in a 6? Answer choice (D), $38.16, has to be the correct answer. Notice that you

could solve this problem without having to calculate the final answer!

Now back to the problem you saw at the beginning of this section:

$356 \times 39 =$

(A) 13,781

(B) 13,723

(C) 13,884

(D) 14,875

(E) 15,233

We know that 6 (from 356) $\times$ 9 (from 39) is 54, which means that the correct answer has to end in a 4. Only choice (C), 13,884, ends in a 4, so it must be the right answer.

Don't forget. Scan the choices, and always check how they end.

MATH STRATEGY 3.
Approximate

Sometimes you don't have to find the exact answer. You can approximate and get away with it. What's even better, if you approximate, you save time. And you can use that extra time on the more difficult problems. Here's an example.

If the weight of 33 boxes is 65 pounds, what is the weight of 49 boxes?

(A) 88

(B) 97

(C) 98

(D) 103

(E) 137

You can do this problem by approximating. Notice that the weight of 33 boxes is just a little less than twice 33, which is 66. This tells you that the weight of one box is a little less than 2 pounds. So 49 boxes must weigh just a little less than $49 \times 2 = 98$ pounds. So choice (C), 98, is too high (because we want our answer to be less than 98), which means that only choice (B), 97, is close enough to be the answer.

So remember, you can save a lot of time if you get in the habit of approximating. Before you work a problem, see if you can approximate your answer. This is a good strategy to use if the five answer choices are not close in value. If the answer choices are spread apart, that tells you that the right answer can be approximated.

MATH STRATEGY 4.
Work from the Choices

In high school, you learned to set up equations whenever you saw a word problem. This may be a good strategy some of the time. But most of the time, there's another strategy that is much faster. Suppose a problem goes like this:

Bill's wallet has $1, $5, and $10 bills. If he has a total of 12 bills, including 6 singles, that add up to $56, how many $10 bills does he have?

(A) 1

(B) 2

(C) 3

(D) 4

(E) 5

One way to do this problem is to set up one equation for the total amount of money that Bill has:

$$S + 5F + 10T = 56$$

where S is the number of singles, F is the number of $5 bills, and T is the number of $10 bills.

Then you'd need another equation for the total number of bills that Bill has:

$$S + F + T = 12$$

And then you have to solve the two equations.

This method works, but it's awfully slow. Here's a better way to do it. The secret is to work from the choices. To work from the choices, always start from choice (C) and then plug the answer back into the problem. So, let's plug in 3 as a possible answer.

Remember, we're looking for the number of $10 bills. Let's suppose Bill has three $10 bills. They total

$30. He also has six singles, and so with three more bills he has nine bills. That means he has to have three $5 bills to get a total of 12 bills. But how do these numbers add up?

$$6 \text{ singles} = \$6$$

$$3 \text{ \$10 bills} = \$30$$

$$3 \text{ \$5 bills} = \$15$$

$$\text{Total} = \$51$$

But this total is not enough, because we need $56. Let's look at the choices again. We know that choice (C) is too low. Zap it. If choice (C) is too low, we know that choices (B) and (A) are also too low. At this point, you should cross off choices (A), (B), and (C). Notice that if you wanted to guess, you now have a 50-50 shot. But let's keep going.

We'll plug in choice (D). If it works, great. If it doesn't work, we know choice (E) has to be the answer. So, let's try choice (D) and plug in 4 as the number of $10 bills that Bill has. If Bill has four $10 bills, then he has ten bills—six singles and four $10 bills. Since he has a total of 12 bills, he must have two $5 bills.

$$6 \text{ singles} = \$6$$

$$4 \text{ \$10 bills} = \$40$$

$$2 \text{ \$5 bills} = \$10$$

$$\text{Total} = \$56$$

This works, and so we know that the right answer is choice (D), 4.

So remember: Whenever you see word problems, consider starting from the answers and working your way back to the problem instead of taking the time to set up and solve equations. When you plug in values, start from choice (C). However, you should be aware of a couple of exceptions to the "start with choice (C)" rule.

Exceptions

If the problem says, "Find the *least* value, the *smallest* angle, or the *lowest* integer," start from the lowest choice, usually choice (A). If the problem says, "Find the *most*, *largest*, or *greatest* value," start from the highest choice, usually choice (E). Here's an example:

What is the lowest positive factor of 24?

(A) 0

(B) 1

(C) 2

(D) 12

(E) 24

Since we're looking for the *lowest* positive factor, we start from choice (A). Is 0 a factor of 24? No. Zap choice (A). Let's look at choice (B), 1. Is 1 a factor of 24? Yes, it is. Is 1 positive? Yes, it is. And so this is the winner. Notice, you don't need to go further. So, remember: Whenever you can, plug in values and work from choices.

MATH STRATEGY 5.

Use Numbers for Unknowns

The people who write tests love things like P's and Q's and R's and X's. They talk about companies that manufacture T garments, about people who are X years older than their brothers, and about Q factors. The best way to make sense out of this weird test language is to say it in English.

To do that, whenever you see P's, Q's, or X's, change them to numbers. Let's look at an example.

If a company produces q items in d days, how many items can it produce in m days?

(A) $\dfrac{qd}{m}$

(B) $\dfrac{dm}{q}$

(C) $\dfrac{qm}{d}$

(D) $\dfrac{d}{qm}$

(E) $\dfrac{m}{qd}$

The easiest way to solve this problem is to change q to an easy number, say 10. Then you can change d days to another easy number, like 1 day, and m to 2 days. Then, the question reads:

If a company produces 10 items in 1 day, how many items can it produce in 2 days?

Now if 10 items are produced in 1 day, it's easy to see that in 2 days, 20 items can be produced. With the values of $q = 10$, $d = 1$, and $m = 2$, see which choice gives you 20.

Choice (A): $\dfrac{10 \times 1}{2} = 5$

Choice (B): $\dfrac{1 \times 2}{10} = \dfrac{1}{5}$

Choice (C): $\dfrac{10 \times 2}{1} = 20$

Choice (C) works. But let's see what happens to the other choices.

Choice (D): $\dfrac{1}{10 \times 2} = \dfrac{1}{20}$

Choice (E): $\dfrac{2}{10 \times 1} = \dfrac{1}{5}$

As you can see, only choice (C) gives 20, and so it is the right answer. So remember, if you find yourself staring at a, b, c, q, r, and so on, just plug in your own numbers for these variables.

Instant Replay: Problem-Solving Strategies

1. Scan the choices.

2. See how it ends.

3. Approximate.

4. Work from the choices.

5. Use numbers for unknowns.

Math Strategies:
Quantitative Comparison and Diagrams

Assignment for Today:

Learn strategies for quantitative comparison and diagram questions.

QUANTITATIVE COMPARISON QUESTIONS

The quantitative comparison (QC) section of your math test looks something like this:

Common Quantity

Quantity in Column A	Quantity in Column B

Your task is to evaluate the quantity in each column to determine which column is greater. Compare the quantities and answer

  (A) if Column A is greater than Column B

  (B) if Column B is greater than Column A

  (C) if Column A is equal to Column B

  (D) if you cannot determine a definite relationship from the information given

  Never answer (E)

Here's an easy example.

Column A	Column B

$$x = 2$$
$$y = 3$$

$x - y$	$y - x$

Notice that Column A is $2 - 3 = -1$, and Column B is $3 - 2 = 1$. This means that Column B is greater than Column A. So on your answer sheet, you should mark B as your answer.

Here are some useful strategies for the QC section.

QC STRATEGY 1.
Substitute Values for Variables

Whenever you see variables like x, y, z, a, b, c, and so on in the QC section of your test, you should immediately start plugging in values for the variables to find out which column is greater.

Make sure that you plug in a wide range of values. First plug in 0 as a value of the variable, and see which column is greater. After that, plug in a positive number (1 is a good one) and then a negative number (–1, for example). If these three different values always give you the same answer, you've probably found the correct answer. However, as soon as you get two different results, you can stop because the right answer is choice (D)—the greater column cannot be determined. Here's an example.

Column A	Column B

$$-3 \leq t \leq 3$$

t^2	t^3

Start by plugging in values for t. We know that t can be 0 because we're told that t can have any value from –3 to 3. So plug in 0 for t. Then we get:

Column A = 0 and Column B = 0.

This tells us that the right answer might be choice (C). But don't stop here. Plug in other values for t. For example, what happens if t is 3?

Column A = 3^2 = 9 and Column B = 3^3 = 27.

Here Column B is greater than Column A. Bingo! We got two different results—first C and now A. This immediately tells us that the correct answer is choice (D), it cannot be determined.

Notice that if you had stopped after plugging in 0 for t, your answer would have been incorrect. It's very important to plug in a wide range of values, including negative numbers.

QC Strategy 2.
Simplify If You Can

The QC questions on your test are designed for speed. The more shortcuts you know, the faster you can do the problems. One important shortcut is simplifying. Whenever you can, you should eliminate common terms before you do fancy computations. Let's take an example. Suppose you are asked to compare the perimeters of the two figures shown.

Column A	Column B

All small triangles are equilateral
with sides of length 1.

Perimeter of figure

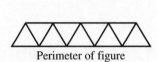
Perimeter of figure

Perimeter simply means the distance around the outer edge of the figure. Before you actually calculate the distances, remember to cross out the number of sides of triangles that are common to Column A and Column B. This means that you should first draw the figure on your scratch paper. For every side that you consider in Column A, cross out a side in Column B. You will see that nine sides are common to both columns. Just cross them out.

Column A	Column B

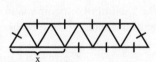

Now you're left with just two sides (marked "x") that remain in Column B. Column B has two extra sides, and so the right answer is choice (B). Notice that it wasn't really necessary to calculate the perimeter of each triangle. Crossing out the same numbers of sides made this an easy problem.

QC Strategy 3.
Factor Out Common Terms

Before you do any calculation, you should first see if common terms can be factored out. You can then eliminate the common terms and simplify your work. Let's compare these two quantities.

Column A	Column B

$$x \neq -7$$
$$x \neq -4$$

$$\boxed{\dfrac{x^2 - 49}{x + 7}} \qquad\qquad \boxed{\dfrac{x^2 - 16}{x + 4}}$$

Did you notice what is common? Let's factor the quantities on the numerator of both fractions. The numerator of Column A, $x^2 - 49$, can be written as:

$$x^2 - 49 = (x + 7)(x - 7)$$

So, Column A can be written as:

$$\frac{x^2 - 49}{x + 7} = \frac{(x+7)(x-7)}{(x+7)} = (x - 7)$$

We can divide the $(x + 7)$ terms from the numerator and denominator to get $(x - 7)$ for Column A.

Similarly, in Column B, $(x^2 - 16)$ can be written as:

$$x^2 - 16 = (x + 4)(x - 4)$$

So, Column B can be written as:

$$\frac{x^2 - 16}{x + 4} = \frac{(x+4)(x-4)}{(x+4)} = (x - 4)$$

We can divide the $(x + 4)$ terms from the numerator and denominator to get $(x - 4)$ for Column B.

So we have $(x - 7)$ in Column A and $(x - 4)$ in Column B. No matter which value is taken by x, we can see that Column B will always be greater than Column A because Column B is only 4 less than x, whereas Column A is 7 less than x.

As you can see, factoring out the common terms will save you lots of time on the exam.

DIAGRAM QUESTIONS

As you well know, it is easy to make careless mistakes on the test. This is especially true if the problem is long and wordy. One good strategy to guard against careless mistakes is to draw the diagram on your scratch paper. On your scratch paper, feel free to mark on the diagram and write down the lengths of lines and values of angles. If no diagram is given to you, see if you can draw one yourself.

Before you work on the following strategies, you should be aware of one special fact about your test: In the QC section of your test, *do not* assume that diagrams are drawn to scale. Angles that look perpendicular are not necessarily perpendicular; in fact, it's very likely that they're *not* perpendicular. Similarly, angles that look parallel may *not* be parallel.

Here are three very useful diagram strategies.

DIAGRAM STRATEGY 1.
Make a Sketch

It's very easy to drown in test language. To keep your head above water, you should get in the habit of drawing a diagram whenever you can. Here's a good example of how a sketch can help:

If the radius of a circle inscribed within a square is 5 feet, what is the perimeter of the square?

This question may look confusing, but it becomes simple if you draw a diagram. Let's see how we might do that.

We know that a circle of radius 5 is inscribed within a square. The diagram you draw may look something like this:

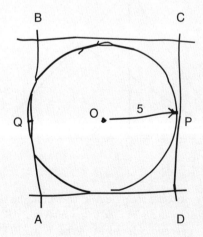

The problem asks you to find the perimeter of square *ABCD*. Because *ABCD* is a square, we know that all four sides have the same length. $\overline{OP}$ is the radius of the circle, and its length is 5. This means that $\overline{OQ}$, which is another radius, also has length 5. So, *QP* = 5 + 5 = 10. If *QP* is 10, then *AD* is also 10. Now we know that one side of the square is 10, which means that all sides of the square are 10. So the perimeter of the square is

Perimeter = *AB* + *BC* + *CD* + *DA* = 10 + 10 + 10 + 10 = 40.

Notice that even though the problem didn't come with a figure, you were able to draw one and simplify your work considerably.

DIAGRAM STRATEGY 2.
Mark Up Given Diagrams

If a problem on your test comes with a diagram, you should get in the habit of drawing it on your scratch paper and marking on it. That way, you minimize your chances of making careless mistakes. Marking on the given diagram also helps you keep focused and saves you time. Here's an example. Suppose a question on your test went something like this:

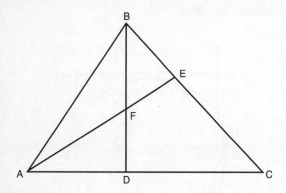

In the isosceles triangle *ABC* shown in the figure, m∠*BAC* = m∠*BCA* = 40°. $\overline{BD}$ bisects ∠*ABC* and $\overline{AE}$ is perpendicular to $\overline{BC}$. What is m∠*BFE*?

We're told that m∠*BAC* is equal to m∠*BCA*, and each one is 40 degrees. We also know that $\overline{BD}$ bisects ∠*ABC*, which means that m∠*ABD* is equal to m∠*DBC*. Also, $\overline{AE}$ is perpendicular to $\overline{BC}$. Let's mark what we know.

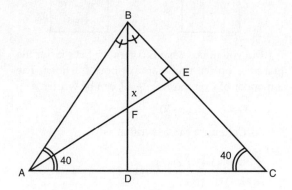

We want to find m∠*BFE*, marked *x* in the figure. First, let's look at triangle *ABC*. If the two bottom angles are each 40 degrees, they add up to 80 degrees, which means m∠*ABC* must be 100 degrees so that the three angles add up to 180 degrees. ∠*ABC* was bisected, so each angle must be 50 degrees.

Now look at triangle *BFE*. We know that m∠*B* = 50 and m∠*E* = 90. Together, they add up to 90 + 50 = 140 degrees. Because the three angles of any triangle must add up to 180 degrees, the measure of ∠*F* must be 180 – 140 = 40 degrees.

DIAGRAM STRATEGY 3.
Distort Given Diagrams

On the GRE, looks can be deceiving. Angles that look equal may not be equal and lines that look parallel may not be parallel. Every time you see two lines that look parallel, you should immediately assume that they're not parallel. In fact, you should distort those lines so that they look anything *but* parallel. In other words, don't hesitate to distort the given diagram. Here's an example.

Column A	Column B

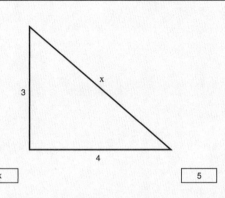

Suppose you're given a triangle as shown here. You're asked to compare the length of the side marked x with 5. So in Column A you have x, and in Column B you have 5.

When you see two sides marked 3 and 4, you might be tempted to think that the third side, x, is 5. Right? x would be 5 if the given triangle were a right triangle. But nothing in the problem says that it is a right triangle. In fact, you should assume that it is *not* a right triangle.

Let's see what happens if we distort the given diagram. Let's assume that the angle that looks like a 90-degree angle is, say, 30 degrees.

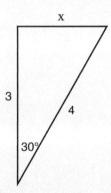

Notice that side x decreases from its original length if the bottom angle is 30 degrees. Similarly, watch what happens if the angle is, say, 120 degrees instead.

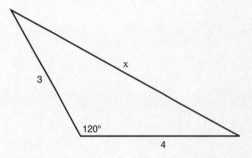

We can see that if the angle is 120 degrees, x becomes longer.

You've probably figured out by now that it's not possible to tell whether x is less than, equal to, or greater than 5, and so the right answer is choice (D), it cannot be determined. By distorting the given diagram, we were able to get the right answer.

Instant Replay: Quantitative Comparison and Diagrams

Quantitative Comparison

1. Substitute values for variables.

2. Simplify if you can.

3. Factor out common terms.

Diagrams

1. Make a sketch.

2. Mark up given diagrams.

3. Distort given diagrams.

Day 7

Introduction to the Writing Assessment and Issue Analysis Strategies

Assignment for Today:

Familiarize yourself with the Writing Assessment section and learn issue analysis strategies.

INTRODUCTION TO THE WRITING ASSESSMENT

The writing assessment is the newest section of the GRE. It asks you to write two essays. In the first essay, you present your perspective on an issue, and in the second, you analyze an argument. These two sections are designed to test your ability to

- Write in standard English
- Present your ideas in a logical and coherent manner
- Think critically and present a set of evidence-based arguments
- Analyze an issue and an argument presented to you

The writing assessment is not designed to test your knowledge in a particular content area. Hence, you will not have an advantage if the topics given to you pertain to your area of expertise. Conversely, you won't be at a disadvantage if you are asked to write about a topic that you know little about. What this means for you is that you should not make as-sumptions about what is not explicitly stated in the passage in front of you. We will return to this point later in the chapter, but first you should familiarize yourself with each of the two sections.

WRITING THE ISSUE ESSAY

ISSUE ANALYSIS STRATEGY 1.
Familiarize Yourself with the Requirements

You will be given two topics, and you will be asked to choose one to write about. In this essay, you have to make an argument for or against a position.

ISSUE ANALYSIS STRATEGY 2.
Time Yourself

You will be given 45 minutes to complete this essay. It is extremely important that you time yourself ac-cordingly. We recommend that you spend no more than 2 minutes deciding which of the two topics you are going to address. Spend another 5 minutes jotting down the main arguments that you will be making. Finally, set aside 5 minutes at the end to revise and edit your work. This means you have roughly 30 to 33 minutes to actually write the essay. As you begin to write, make sure you check your watch periodically to determine how much more time you have left.

ISSUE ANALYSIS STRATEGY 3.
Organize Before You Write

Here are a number of steps we recommend you take before you actually begin writing.

1. Decide which position you're going to adopt. You can take any of these approaches:

   a) Agree completely with the stated claim. If you choose this option, make sure you provide lots of supporting arguments and examples. Remember, however, that examples should not be the sole evidence for the position you adopt. Rather, examples should be used to support the argument that you make for the position that you adopt.

   b) Agree only partially with the stated claim. For example, you might want to qualify the claim such that only under particular circumstances would you expect the claim to be true. Make sure you specify what those circumstances are.

   c) Disagree with the stated claim. If you choose this option, make sure you present strong evidence for, or examples that illustrate, the other side of the argument.

   d) Question the validity of the underlying assumptions. Point out what the underlying assumptions are and discuss why they cannot be accepted.

2. On scratch paper, write down the four or five main arguments that you will be making in your essay. Don't try to come up with more than four or five arguments—you're not going to have enough time to make a case for more than five arguments. It is better to provide few, but compelling, arguments than to provide more than what you can reasonably discuss.

3. Order your arguments in a logical way and determine what kinds of evidence you will provide to support your arguments. It's good to begin and end with your best arguments.

4. Think of examples. And more examples.

ISSUE ANALYSIS STRATEGY 4.
Be Clear about the Main Point

Your issue essay has to make an overall point—it has to have a "take-home" message. Your reader won't be able to identify your main point unless you yourself are clear about what it is. So, make sure that everything you mention in your essay supports this main point. This point should form your conclusion.

ISSUE ANALYSIS STRATEGY 5.
Know the Pool of Possible Topics

ETS has published a complete pool of issue essay topics (go to http://www.gre.org/issuetop.html for a complete list). Familiarize yourself with them. The topics that you will encounter on the GRE will be taken from this pool.

Practice Example 1

Here is a practice example. Let's assume that the topic is:

> "The stability of an organization is determined by how it responds to unusual events."

Before you actually write your issue analysis, we would like you to do the following exercise. First, decide what your position is going to be (for, against, qualified support, question the underlying assumptions, or a combination), and underline the appropriate choice:

<u>Your position</u> (underline one or more):

| | | Qualified | Question |
| Support | Oppose | support | assumption |

Now write down five points that you will make, and note examples whenever you can:

1. _____

2. _____

3. _____

4. _____

5. _____

Next, renumber the arguments (to the left) so that you begin and end with your strongest points. After you feel comfortable with the sequence, begin writing your position paper. Then, turn the page to see how we have approached the task.

Notes for Sample Response

"The stability of an organization is determined by how it responds to unusual events."

Your position (underline one or more):

Support   <u>Oppose</u>   Qualified support   <u>Question assumption</u>

As you can see, we have decided to oppose the position and question some underlying assumptions.

Now write down five points that you will make, and note examples whenever you can:

1. False assumption: stable organization is desirable.

2. False assumption: organizations have a unified response.

3. "Unusual" events, by definition, are rare.

4. It's the response to usual, everyday events that is more meaningful.

5. Some degree of stability is required.

Now that we have all the points, we are in a position to write our essay. Here's what a sample essay might look like.

Sample Essay

The given proposition is based on the assumption that stability in organizations is a desirable outcome. Whether or not this proposition is true depends on what one means by stability. If stability means predictability, it may certainly be a desirable characteristic of organizations, as it allows its internal (e.g., employees) and external (creditors) constituents to make long-term plans. If, however, stability refers to a lack of needed change and a preference for the status quo, it can be deadly for an organization, especially given the rapid change in technology that we are currently witnessing.

The phrase "how it responds" is also based on the assumption that organizations respond in one particular (or identifiable) way. Organizational responses are seldom unidimensional, even though they may appear so. Responses to any event typically are multifaceted: When a crisis occurs, one part of the organization (e.g., the investment-oriented sector) may respond in one way, while another part of the organization (e.g., public relations) may respond in a radically different way. Moreover, these different responses may be at odds with each other so that the net effect, when viewed from the outside, may appear to be no response at all.

Unusual events, by definition, are rare, which means that they are not representative of the normal state of affairs. It is far more important for organizations to worry about how they manage the day-to-day (i.e., usual) events simply because these events happen more often and more people are affected by them. Unusual events, because of their rarity, are not going to affect as many people. Besides, people are willing to forgive an organization if it makes a mistake in its response to unusual events. They are less forgiving, however, if an organization is perceived not to know how to respond to frequently occurring events whose effects can be cumulative.

Finally, there is no question that organizations need some degree of stability, and during times of crisis, organizations need to demonstrate that they are capable of restoring order and maintaining a certain degree of continuity. For this to happen, organizations need to have contingency plans in place.

Overall, organizations need to be concerned much more with day-to-day, normal events than unusual events. It is the manner in which organizations respond to normal events that determines the organization's predictability and ultimately its long-term survival and growth.

A few points about the essay you just read:

- Notice that each paragraph addresses one argument.

- Your essay can adopt a position that both supports and opposes the main premise.

- A conclusion summarizes the overall position.

Before you actually write the essay, we recommend that you browse the different issue analysis topics presented on the ETS Web site (http://www.gre.org/issuetop.html) and go through the exercise of jotting down your main ideas (as we did above). After working on a few examples, you'll soon discover the pattern that works best for you. Follow the same pattern in your exam.

Practice Example 2

Let us suppose that this is the topic you are given:

"Some people argue that political campaigns should be publicly financed, whereas others argue that the government should not provide funds for political campaigns. What position(s) do you support and why?"

Here is another, slightly modified approach that you might adopt.

Your position (underline one or more):

| | | Qualified | Question |
| Support | Oppose | support | assumption |

Now write down points that you will make, and note examples whenever you can:

1. _____

2. _____

3. _____

4. _____

5. _____

Next, renumber the arguments (above) so that you begin and end with your strongest points. After you feel comfortable with the sequence, begin writing your issue essay. Then, turn the page to see how we have approached the task.

Notes for Sample Response

"Some people argue that political campaigns should be publicly financed, whereas others argue that the government should not provide funds for political campaigns. What position(s) do you support and why?"

<u>Your position</u> (underline one or more):

		Qualified	Question
<u>Support</u>	Oppose	support	assumption

As you can see, we have decided to support the position that publicly financing political campaigns is a good idea.

Now write down points that you will make, and note examples whenever you can:

1. Level playing field

2. Lesser need to raise money

3. Private citizens have greater say

Now you are in a position to write the essay. In the essay, you would argue that: (1) We would level the playing field so that wealthy individuals would not have an unfair advantage. (2) Incumbent politicians would not have to worry about raising money and instead they could concentrate on their jobs. (3) Because politicians would not have to court money from industry, they would listen to individual citizens as much as they do now to industry.

For each of these arguments, provide evidence or examples. For argument (1), you could discuss that, in the current system, individuals who are not wealthy but who have sound ideas are discouraged from running for public office because of the immense expenses required to do so. For argument (2), you could argue why the current system favors incumbents and why incumbents have to spend so much of their time raising money. Similarly, for argument (3), you could discuss why individual citizens, compared with industry lobbyists, do not currently enjoy the same attention from their elected officials. What does this mean for democracy?

The important point here is that you should first frame the issue in broad terms, then provide concrete examples to make each individual argument, and then provide a summary of your position.

Day 8

Argument Analysis Strategies

Assignment for Today:

Familiarize yourself with the argument analysis strategies.

ARGUMENT ANALYSIS STRATEGY 1.

Familiarize Yourself with the Requirements

For this section, you will be given a passage that contains an argument. Your task is to critique the argument by commenting on the quality of the points made and the soundness of the conclusion that is drawn from the points. Notice that, unlike the issue task, you will not be given a choice of topics. Total time: 30 minutes.

ARGUMENT ANALYSIS STRATEGY 2.

Time Yourself

Because you're only given 30 minutes, you need to be careful about pacing yourself. We recommend that you set aside 5 minutes at the end to edit your work. Spend about 10 minutes listing your arguments. This will leave you about 15 minutes to actually write your essay. Make sure you check your watch periodically so that you don't run out of time unexpectedly.

ARGUMENT ANALYSIS STRATEGY 3.

Identify the Assumptions

One of the best ways to critique an argument is to poke holes in the assumptions that underlie the argument. Assumptions are not explicitly stated. Rather, they are implied. They are the author's way of saying: "Grant me the following premises. Let's assume for a second that they are true." Your first task is to identify the assumptions in the passage. Here is an example. See if you can determine what the underlying assumptions are.

> "Automobile accidents can be drastically reduced through rigorous enforcement of laws against drunk driving. After Massachusetts began cracking down on drunk drivers two years ago, the state's highway fatalities dropped by 30 percent."

Here are a few assumptions on which the passage rests:

1. There are currently effective laws against drunk driving.

2. Current laws are not being rigorously enforced.

3. Massachusetts is representative of most other places.

4. During the period of tougher enforcement, nothing else related to automobile accident rates was happening in Massachusetts.

5. Cracking down on drunk drivers won't create other problems.

ARGUMENT ANALYSIS STRATEGY 4.
Poke Holes in the Assumptions

Now that we have identified the assumptions, we can begin tearing them down. Here is an example of how this may be done.

Assumption 1: There are currently effective laws against drunk driving.

You may argue that more rigorous enforcement of effective laws works only in states where such laws exist and that in states where such laws don't exist, the solution is to create these laws.

Assumption 2: Current laws are not being rigorously enforced.

You may argue that current laws are selectively enforced, either during particular times in the year (e.g., during holidays) or in selected neighborhoods.

Assumption 3: Massachusetts is representative of most other places.

Just because the program worked in Massachusetts doesn't mean it will work in other places. Perhaps there is something unique about Massachusetts. Or, maybe because the state was trying a new strategy, there was a lot of media publicity surrounding the enforcement program, which made drunk drivers stay off the streets.

Assumption 4: During the period of tougher enforcement, nothing else related to automobile accident rates was happening in Massachusetts.

Perhaps something else was happening in Massachusetts at the same time that was responsible for the reduction in drunk-driving accidents. For example, it could be that the state imposed higher taxes on alcohol, which reduced consumption.

Assumption 5: Cracking down on drunk drivers won't create other problems.

If more police resources are spent cracking down on drunk driving, fewer resources will be available to enforce other laws (e.g., against crime), which could mean that reducing drunk-driving problems will exacerbate other kinds of problems.

ARGUMENT ANALYSIS STRATEGY 5.
Identify and Challenge the Conclusion

All argument analysis passages come with some kind of conclusion. For example, in the passage we just analyzed, the conclusion is that tougher enforcement will reduce automobile accidents. Your task is to identify the conclusion and then see if it follows logically from the arguments that are presented. Here's another example:

> "Even though cars today are far more efficient in their gasoline consumption than they were at any time in the past, our reliance on foreign oil continues to increase. In order to reduce this reliance, we need to increase our domestic oil exploration efforts."

The conclusion of the passage above is that we need to increase our domestic oil exploration efforts. You can challenge this conclusion in a number of ways. For example, you might argue that we can explore all we want, but if there isn't any more domestic oil, then the problem won't be solved. Or, you might argue that the best way to reduce our reliance on foreign oil is to reduce the number of cars on the road, to reduce the number of trucks, or to seek alternative fuels.

ARGUMENT ANALYSIS STRATEGY 6.
Organize Before You Write

Before writing your essay, we recommend that you take a minute to list the assumptions and/or conclusions in the given passage. Then, you will be in a better position to analyze the passage more critically. One way of organizing your thoughts is to simply make a chart. For example, your chart might look something like this:

Assumption 1: _____

Assumption 2: _____

Assumption 3: _____

Conclusion 1: _____

Conclusion 2: _____

   Once you've identified the assumptions and conclusions, you can then draw arrows to connect one idea with another. As an example, consider the following passage. After reading the passage, identify some assumptions and conclusions.

"Because working mothers are not allowed enough time off from their jobs, we are fast developing into a society that neglects its children. As the number of working women in our society has steadily increased in the last two decades, the number of neglected children has also increased. Many women work outside the home because of necessity, and hence we cannot lay the blame on these women. Rather, the blame lies with corporations that do not allow their employees sufficient flexibility in managing their time to take care of their young children. For this reason, the government needs to enact laws that would allow working parents to take time off to care for their young children without fear of losing their jobs."

Assumption 1: _____

Assumption 2: _____

Assumption 3: _____

Conclusion 1: _____

Conclusion 2: _____

   After you have filled in the assumption(s) and conclusion(s), see the next page for some suggestions.

Sample Assumptions and Conclusions

Here is a sample of the assumptions and conclusions you might have extracted from the passage.

Assumption 1: Mothers are neglecting their children.

Assumption 2: There is a direct correlation between longer work hours for mothers and society's neglect of children.

Assumption 3: Companies don't allow parents time off.

Assumption 4: The extra time that parents would have (under the proposed solution) would be spent with the children.

Assumption 5: Fathers don't need to shoulder the burden.

Conclusion: Stricter laws will solve the problem.

There are many more assumptions, of course, but the ones identified here can certainly provide you with enough ammunition to write a critical analysis. Notice that once you get into the habit of identifying the underlying assumptions, responding to the given argument becomes much easier.

ARGUMENT ANALYSIS STRATEGY 7.
Know the Pool of Possible Topics

ETS has published a complete pool of argument analysis topics (go to http://www.gre.org/argutop.html for a complete list). Familiarize yourself with it. The topics that you will encounter on the GRE will be taken from this pool.

Practice Example

How would you respond to the following passage?

The Endangered Species Act has resulted in a remarkable turnaround in the bald eagle population. Whereas, before the Act was implemented, there were an average of 400 sightings of the species per year, these days that number has soared to almost 3,000. This success has also been duplicated in the comeback of whales.

Notice that the author starts with the conclusion that the Endangered Species Act has been successful. The logic for this argument (or the evidence on which this conclusion is built) is that the bald eagle and whale population has been rising. Furthermore, evidence that the bald eagle population has been rising is based on the assumption that the number of sightings is equivalent to the total population. There is no evidence provided to support the claim that the population of the whale has been rising.

Let's start with the assumption. Can we assume that the number of sightings is equivalent to the total population? What if, because of the Act, people became more aware about the bald eagle's existence and so more and more people started looking for them? Or, perhaps binoculars and other detecting devices have become more sophisticated over the years and so more sightings are reported. Or, perhaps the bald eagle now flies closer to more densely populated areas of the country.

Even if we were to assume that the number of sightings is equivalent to the total population, and further that the population of the bald eagle has been rising, do we have enough evidence to support the conclusion that the Act has been successful? What if the rise in the bald eagle population came at the expense of the disappearance of other endangered species?

Finally, notice that no evidence is provided for the increase in the whale population. What if this is also based on the idea that more whales are now sighted?

Once you develop the habit of analyzing the passage in this way, writing this section should be fairly mechanical.

Day 9   to   Day 22

TEST 1

Questions and Answers

Explanations and Strategies

Test 1, Part 1: Math (1).

Questions and Answers

Assignment for Today:

Take the first part of a practice GRE Math Test under actual test conditions. Allow yourself exactly 30 minutes to complete the 30 questions in this test.

Directions: For questions 1–15, each question contains two quantities—one on the left (Column A) and one on the right (Column B). Compare the quantities and answer

(A) if Column A is greater than Column B

(B) if Column B is greater than Column A

(C) if the two columns are equal

(D) if you cannot determine a definite relationship from the information given

Never answer (E)

In some questions, information appears centered between the two columns. Centered information concerns each of the columns for that question only. Any symbol in one column represents the same value if it appears in the other column.

Column A	Column B

1. $\left(\sqrt{20}\right)\left(\sqrt{5}\right)-\left(\sqrt{2}\right)\left(\sqrt{8}\right)$ | $\left(\sqrt{50}\right)\left(\sqrt{2}\right)-\left(\sqrt{6}\right)\left(\sqrt{6}\right)$

2. Interest owed on a loan of \$6,000 at an annual rate of 10%. | Interest owed on a loan of \$12,000 at an annual rate of 5%.

Stefan misread a math problem and took the square root of x when he should have taken the square of x. His answer was a positive integer. Maria did the same problem correctly.

3. (Maria's answer)$^{\frac{1}{2}}$ | (Stefan's answer)^2

Column A	Column B		Column A	Column B

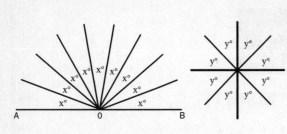

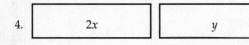

AOB is a line segment

4. $2x$ | y

Each boxer in the Lightweight category weighs 150 pounds or less. The average weight of 4 Lightweight boxers is 140 pounds, and the combined weight of 2 of them is 290 pounds.

5. Weight, in pounds, of the lightest possible of the 4 Lightweight boxers | 120 pounds

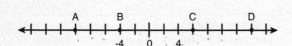

Assume the tick marks are equally spaced.

6. $\dfrac{A+C}{B+D}$ | $\dfrac{2}{5}$

3 balanced coins are tossed at the same time.

7. Probability of getting 2 heads and a tail | Probability of getting only 1 head

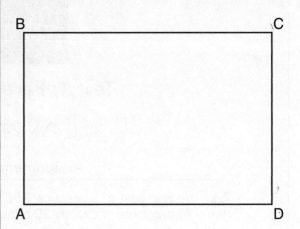

Perimeter of the rectangle *ABCD* is 24, and *AD* is twice *CD*.

8. CD^2 | AD

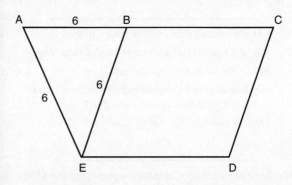

Perimeter of parallelogram *BCDE* = 30.

9. Area of *BCDE* | $27\sqrt{3}$

Column A	Column B		Column A	Column B

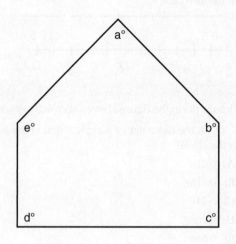

Note: Figure not drawn to scale.

$$a = b = c$$
$$d = \frac{a+b+c}{2}$$
$$e = 2d$$

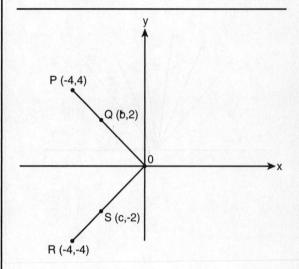

12. | $b + c$ | -4 |

10. | c | 72 |

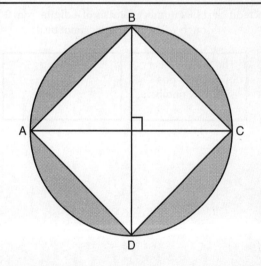

$x < y \le 1$

11. | $x^2 - y^3$ | $x^3 - y^2$ |

$\overline{AC}$ and $\overline{BD}$ are perpendicular bisectors of each other.

Radius of circle = 5.

13. | Area of shaded portion | 25 |

Column A	Column B

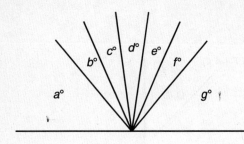

$$a = g$$

$$b = c = d = e = f$$

$$a = 3d$$

14.	$a + b$	65

A credit card PIN number consists of 4 digits from 0 through 9. The first digit cannot be 0.

15.	The total number of different possible PIN numbers.	9^4

Directions: *Solve each problem and select the appropriate answer choice.*

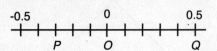

16. Tick marks in the figure above are equally spaced. If $\overline{PQ}$ is the diameter of a circle, what is the area of the circle?

(A) 0.01π

(B) 0.016π

(C) 0.04π

(D) 0.16π

(E) 0.64π

17. Three boxes—A, B, and C—together weigh 26 pounds. Box A weighs one third as much as box B, and box C weighs three times as much as box B. How many pounds does box B weigh?

(A) 2

(B) $3\dfrac{5}{7}$

(C) 6

(D) $8\dfrac{2}{3}$

(E) 13

18. If $\sqrt{y} = 9$, then $y^2 - \sqrt{y} =$

(A) $\sqrt{3} - 9$

(B) 0

(C) $9 - \sqrt{3}$

(D) 6,552

(E) 6,561

19. What is the value of $(p + p^2 + p^4 + q^3)$ when $p = -1$?

   (A) 0

   (B) q^3

   (C) $p + q^3$

   (D) $(1 + q)^3$

   (E) $1 + q^3$

20. If $\dfrac{x+3}{6} = \dfrac{12}{x+4}$, what is the positive value of x?

   (A) 2

   (B) 3

   (C) 5

   (D) $\sqrt{60}$

   (E) 12

Directions: Questions 21–25 are based on the given figure.

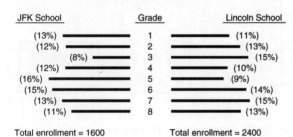

Distribution of Students at JFK School
and Lincoln School by Grade, 1984

21. How many students in JFK School are in 5th and 6th grades combined?

   (A) 240

   (B) 256

   (C) 310

   (D) 496

   (E) 552

22. How many grades in JFK School have more than or equal to the number of students in Lincoln School's 4th grade?

   (A) 1

   (B) 2

   (C) 4

   (D) 7

   (E) 8

23. How many students in Lincoln School are in 6th through 8th grades?

   (A) 42

   (B) 360

   (C) 624

   (D) 768

   (E) 1,008

24. If 100 more students get enrolled in JFK School's 6th grade, and the number of students in other grades doesn't change, what percent of JFK's new total enrollment would be 6th graders?

   (A) 17.44

   (B) 18.17

   (C) 20.00

   (D) 21.25

   (E) 22.25

25. If JFK School's enrollment increases by 400 students, and Lincoln School's enrollment increases by 100 students, then JFK School's proportion of the two schools' total enrollment increases by approximately what percent?

   (A) 4

   (B) 7

   (C) 9

   (D) 20

   (E) 44

Directions: Solve each problem and select the appropriate answer choice, A–E. Circle the letter of your choice.

26. How many 4-digit numbers are there that consist of only *odd* digits?

    (A) 20

    (B) 625

    (C) 1,024

    (D) 4,500

    (E) 5,000

27. For some integer m, let $\{m\}$ be defined by the equation $\{m\} = m\,(1 - m)$. If $n + 1 = \{n + 1\}$, then $n =$

    (A) −2

    (B) −1

    (C) 0

    (D) 1

    (E) 2

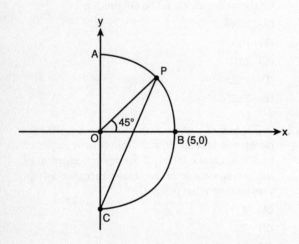

28. In the figure above, ABC is a semicircle with its center at the origin. What is the area of triangle OPC?

    (A) $\dfrac{25}{4}$

    (B) $\dfrac{25}{4}\left(\sqrt{2}+1\right)$

    (C) $\dfrac{25}{2\sqrt{2}}$

    (D) $\dfrac{25}{2}$

    (E) $\dfrac{25}{\sqrt{2}}$

29. Box A and box B have 6 cards each. Each card is marked with one integer, 1 through 6. Both boxes can have more than one card with the same integer, but the sum of all the integers in each box must be 18. Two of the cards in box A are 6's and two of the cards in box B are 5's. If one card is drawn from box A and one from box B but neither a 6 nor a 5 is drawn, what is the *largest* possible sum of the integers on the cards drawn from the two boxes?

    (A) 3

    (B) 4

    (C) 7

    (D) 8

    (E) 12

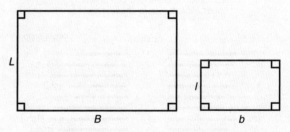

30. In the figure above, the ratio of the perimeter of the larger rectangle to the perimeter of the smaller rectangle is p. If $\dfrac{L-B}{l-b} = d$, what is $\dfrac{L^2-B^2}{l^2-b^2}$ in terms of p and d?

    (A) $p \times d$

    (B) $\dfrac{p}{d}$

    (C) $\dfrac{p^2-d^2}{p^2+d^2}$

    (D) $\dfrac{p+d}{p-d}$

    (E) $p - d^2$

Quick Answer Guide

Test 1, Part 1: Math (1)

1. A	9. C	17. C	25. C
2. D	10. C	18. D	26. B
3. C	11. D	19. E	27. B
4. B	12. C	20. C	28. C
5. C	13. A	21. D	29. C
6. B	14. A	22. B	30. A
7. C	15. A	23. E	
8. A	16. D	24. C	

For explanations to these questions, see Day 10.

Day 10

Test 1, Part 1: Math (1).

Explanations and Strategies

Assignment for Today:

Review the explanations for the Math Test you took on Day 9.

---

1. The correct answer is (A).

As with most quantitative comparison problems, there are at least two ways to work to an answer: in this case, a fast way and a faster way! One fast way is to multiply the square roots in parentheses. So, in Column (A), you get $\sqrt{100} - \sqrt{16}$, which equals 10 – 4, or 6. In Column (B), you get $\sqrt{100} - \sqrt{36}$, which equals 10 – 6, or 4. So Column (A) is greater.

A faster way is to realize that the first set of parentheses is the same for each column (they both equal $\sqrt{100}$). So all you have to do is compare the second sets of parentheses: In Column (A), you have $-\sqrt{16}$, which equals –4. In Column (B), you have $-\sqrt{36}$, which equals –6. Since –4 is greater than –6, Column (A) is greater. (Don't forget about those negative signs!)

2. The correct answer is (D).

The formula for finding interest is:

Interest = Loan amount × rate × time

Notice that we are given the loan amount ($6,000 for Column A and $12,000 for Column B) and the annual rate (10% in Column A and 5% in Column B), but we don't know anything about the time period. For example, the loan in Column A may be for 5 years and the loan in Column B may be for just one month. We just don't know. So, the answer is choice (D).

3. The correct answer is (C).

To solve this problem, let's plug in values for the unknowns. Let's assume that x is 25. Then, Stefan took the square root of 25, which means his answer was 5. Then Column B is:

(Stefan's answer)$^2 = 5^2 = 25$.

The correct answer required Maria to square x. So, with x as 25, Maria's answer was 25 × 25. Then, Column A is:

$$(25 \times 25)^{\frac{1}{2}} = \sqrt{25 \times 25} = 25$$

So, both columns are equal.

4. The correct answer is (B).

Let's look at Column A first. We know that AOB is a straight line, which means that the total angle enclosed by AOB is 180 degrees. There are 9 angles, each x degrees. So each x is $180 \div 9 = 20$ degrees.

So, if $x = 20, 2x = 40$.

Then, Column A $= 40$.

The 8 equal angles in Column B form a circle. We know that a circle has 360 degrees. So, if $8y = 360$, $y = 360 \div 8 = 45$.

Then, Column B $= 45$.

So, Column B is greater than Column A.

5. The correct answer is (C).

We should work with total weights and not with average weights because averages have to be added with caution. We know that the average weight of the 4 boxers is 140 pounds. This means the total weight of the 4 boxers is $140 \times 4 = 560$. (Remember, total weight is the average times the number of boxers.)

We know that two of the boxers have a combined weight of 290 pounds. The heaviest possible weight that any boxer can have is 150 pounds. This means the lighter of the two can weigh a minimum of $290 - 150 = 140$ pounds. Now let's find the lighter of the *other* two boxers.

We know that four of them weigh 560 pounds and two of them weigh 290 pounds. Then, the other two must weigh $560 - 290 = 270$ pounds. Again, the lighter of these 2 boxers can weigh a minimum of $270 - 150 = 120$ pounds.

In both groups of two, to find the lighter boxer, we assume that the heavier boxer weighs the maximum possible amount, which is 150 pounds. This is the only way to make sure that the lighter boxer has the least possible weight.

So, Column A is 120 pounds, which is equal to Column B.

6. The correct answer is (B).

We can determine the coordinates of the points we are interested in by just using the number line. Note that each tick mark is 2 units long.

$$\left.\begin{array}{l} A = -10 \\ B = -4 \\ C = 6 \\ D = 14 \end{array}\right\} \Rightarrow \frac{A + C}{B + D} = \frac{-10 + 6}{-4 + 14} = \frac{-4}{10} = -\frac{2}{5}$$

So, Column A is a negative value and Column B is a positive value, which means Column B is greater than Column A.

7. The correct answer is (C).

If we toss 3 coins, these are the different outcomes:

Coin 1	Coin 2	Coin 3

We notice that there are a total of eight possible outcomes: HHH, HHT, HTH, HTT, THH, THT, TTH, and TTT.

There are three outcomes with two heads and a tail (HHT, HTH, and THH), and so the probability is 3/8, which is Column A.

There are three outcomes with only one head (HTT, THT, and TTH) and so the probability is 3/8, which is Column B.

The two probabilities are equal, and so the answer is choice (C).

8. The correct answer is (A).

We are told that the perimeter is 24. Then, the sum of the length and width is 12 (because the perimeter is twice the sum of the length and width). That is,

$AD + CD = 12$

But, AD is twice CD. That is, $AD = 2(CD)$. So, let's plug in this value of AD in the equation. We get

$$2(CD) + CD = 12$$

Or $$3\,CD = 12$$

that is, $CD = 4$. If CD is 4, AD has to be 8. Then Column A = $4^2 = 16$ and Column B = 8.

So, Column A is greater.

9. The correct answer is (C).

To find the area of the parallelogram $BCDE$, we need its base, ED, and its height. Side BE is 6. Then, side CD is also 6 (in a parallelogram, opposite sides are equal). Together, these two sides sum to 12. We know the perimeter of $BCDE$ is 30. If two of the sides

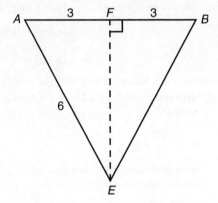

add up to 12, the other two sides must add up to $30 - 12 = 18$. So, side BC must be 9 and the base, ED, must also be 9. Got base, need height.

On to triangle ABE. It has the same height as the parallelogram. Each side of the triangle is equal in length, so it's an equilateral triangle.

We can draw a perpendicular from E to $\overline{AB}$. Then, $AF = BF = 3$. Then, from the right triangle AFE, we can find FE by using the Pythagorean theorem:

$$AE^2 = AF^2 + FE^2$$

Or, $$6^2 = 3^2 + FE^2$$

Or, $$27 = FE^2$$

So, $$FE = \sqrt{27} = \sqrt{9 \times 3} = 3\sqrt{3}$$

So, the height of the parallelogram is $3\sqrt{3}$. We know its base is 9. Then, its area = base × height.

$$= 9 \times 3\sqrt{3} = 27\sqrt{3}$$

So, Column A is equal to Column B.

10. The correct answer is (C).

First, let's find the sum of all interior angles of the given figure. The sum of the interior angles of a polygon is $180 \times (n - 2)$, where n is the number of sides. For example, in a triangle (the number of sides is 3 and so n is 3), the sum of the angles is $180 \times (3 - 2) = 180 \times 1 = 180$.

So, the sum of the interior angles of the figure shown (with 5 sides) is: $180 \times (5 - 2) = 180 \times 3 = 540$.

We're asked to compare the value of angle c with 72 degrees. Let's suppose that c is 72 degrees. Let's see what happens if we plug this value back into the problem.

If c is 72, then $a = 72$ and $b = 72$ (because we're told: $a = b = c$).

We also know that $d = \dfrac{a+b+c}{2}$. If $a, b,$ and c are each 72, then $d = \dfrac{72 + 72 + 72}{2} = \dfrac{216}{2} = 108$.

And, we know that $e = 2d$. So, if $d = 108$, then $e = 2 \times 108 = 216$.

Now, let's add up these values and see if they give us a total of 540 degrees.

$$a + b + c = 216$$
$$d = 108$$
$$e = 216$$

Then, total = 540

So, the value of c is 72 degrees, and the two columns are equal.

11. The correct answer is (D).

The best way to solve this problem is to plug in values for x and y. Let's try the greatest possible value for y, which is 1, and 0 for x (which must be less than y).

Then, Column A = $0 - 1 = -1$,

and Column B = $0 - 1 = -1$.

This implies that the two columns are equal. Now, let's try $x = -1$ and $y = 0$.

Then, Column A = $1 - 0 = 1$,

and Column B = $-1 - 0 = -1$.

Here, Column A is greater.

Because we get two different values, the correct choice is (D).

12. The correct answer is (C).

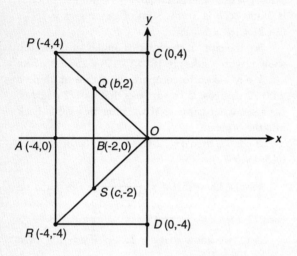

Let's first find the slopes of $\overline{OP}$ and $\overline{OR}$. A slope is simply the ratio of the y-distance to the x-distance. From point O to point P, there is a y-distance of 4 (shown as $\overline{OC}$), and there is an x-distance of –4 (shown as $\overline{OA}$).

Then, slope of $\overline{OP} = \frac{y\text{ - distance}}{x\text{ - distance}} = \frac{4}{-4} = -1$

This means, along the entire line $\overline{OP}$, if we move 1 to the left, we have to move 1 upward. Notice that to get to point Q, we need to move 2 upward from the origin. This means we have to move $-1 \times 2 = -2$ on the x-axis. So, $b = -2$.

The slope of line $\overline{OR}$ is $\frac{y\text{ - distance}}{x\text{ - distance}} = \frac{-4}{-4} = 1$

This means, along line $\overline{OR}$, if we move 1 to the left, we have to move 1 downward. To get to point S, we move 2 downward from the origin. So, we also need to move 2 to the left, which means the value of c is –2.

So, $b = -2$ and $c = -2$. Then, $b + c = -2 + -2$
        $= -4$, and the two columns are equal.

13. The correct answer is (A).

To find the area of the shaded portion, first let's find the area of the circle. Once we find the area of the circle, we can subtract from it the area of rectangle $ABCD$ (because everything is symmetrical, angle $A =$ angle $B =$ angle $C =$ angle D, and so $ABCD$ is a rectangle), and we'll be left with the area of the shaded portion.

Area of circle $= \pi r^2 = \pi(5^2) = 25\pi$

Notice that rectangle $ABCD$ can be divided into four right triangles, each with height = base = radius $= 5$

Then,   area of each triangle $= \frac{1}{2}$ base $\times$ height

$= \frac{1}{2}$ radius $\times$ radius

$= \frac{1}{2}(5 \times 5) = \frac{25}{2}$

There are four such triangles in rectangle $ABCD$.

So,   area of rectangle $ABCD = 4 \times$ area of each triangle

$= 4 \times \frac{25}{2} = 50$

So,   area of shaded portion = area of circle – area of $ABCD$

$= 25\pi - 50$

We have to compare this quantity in Column A with 25 in Column B. Notice that 25π is more than 75 because the value of π is a little more than 3 (it's roughly 3.14). We can approximate 25π to 78 or so. So, the area of the shaded portion is about 78 – 50, which is about 28. No matter what its exact value, the area of the shaded portion is going to be more than 25, and so Column A is greater.

14. The correct answer is (A).

To solve this problem, we need to find the value of a and b. We see that all angles add up to 180° because they form a straight line.

So, $a + b + c + d + e + f + g = 180$

Let's rewrite this equation using only a and b, because we need to compare $a + b$ in Column A with 65 in Column B.

Then, we can write $c = b$, $d = b$, $e = b$, $f = b$, and $g = a$.

So, $a + b + c + d + e + f + g = 180$ can be written as:

$a + b + b + b + b + b + a = 180$

Or, $2a + 5b = 180$

We also know that $a = 3d$ and $d = b$. So, $a = 3b$.

Then,	$2(3b) + 5b$	$= 180$
Or,	$6b + 5b$	$= 180$
Or,	$11b$	$= 180$
Or,	b	$= \dfrac{180}{11}$
Because	$a = 3b, a$	$= \dfrac{180}{11} \times 3$

To get the value of $a + b$, we note that a is $3\left(\dfrac{180}{11}\right)$ and b is $1\left(\dfrac{180}{11}\right)$. So, together, $a + b = 4\left(\dfrac{180}{11}\right) = \dfrac{720}{11}$.

If you divide this expression, you will find that it is 65 plus some (we don't need the exact amount; we only need to know that it's a bit more than 65). So Column A is 65 plus some and Column B is 65. The answer then is choice (A).

15. The correct answer is (A).

Column A first. A PIN number has four positions and has a number in each position. In all positions except the first one, there are 10 possible numbers (0 through 9) that can fill that position. In the first position, since 0 is not allowed, there are nine possible choices. To get the total number of possible PIN numbers, we multiply these numbers together:

9 possibilities in the first position

× 10 possibilities in the 2nd position

× 10 possibilities in the 3rd position

× 10 possibilities in the 4th position

= 9,000 total possibilities.

There are a couple of ways that we can see that 9,000 is greater than 9^4, the quantity in Column B. We could compute 9^4 directly (yuck) and see that it is less than 9,000 ($9^4 = 6,561$), or we could express Column A as 9×10^3 and Column B as 9×9^3, and choose Column A because $10^3 > 9^3$.

16. The correct answer is (D). 0.16π

We're told that $\overline{PQ}$ is the diameter of the circle. We should first find the length of the diameter. From the

figure, we know that PQ is the sum of PO and OQ. PO is 0.3 (notice it's not -0.3 because distances cannot be negative) and OQ is 0.5. So, the diameter of the circle is $0.3 + 0.5 = 0.8$.

If the diameter is 0.8, the radius is half that, or 0.4.

If the radius is 0.4, the area $= \pi r^2 = \pi(0.4)^2 = 0.16\pi$.

17. The correct answer is (C). 6

Word problems like these are best solved by plugging in the answer choices. As usual, we start from choice (C), 6. Because the question asked for the weight of box B, we plug in 6 pounds as its weight.

We're told that box C weighs 3 times as much as box B. So, if box B weighs 6 pounds, box C weighs 6 × 3 = 18 pounds. Now, box A weighs one third as much as box B. So, if box B weighs 6 pounds, box A must weigh $\frac{1}{3} \times 6 = 2$ pounds.

Then,	weight of box A	=	2 pounds,
	weight of box B	=	6 pounds,
and	weight of box C	=	18 pounds.
Then,	the total weight = 26 pounds, which works, and so choice (C) is the right answer.		

18. The correct answer is (D). 6,552

Let's start with what we know. We know that $\sqrt{y} = 9$. Then, if we square both sides of this equation, $y = 81$.

Let's square this one more time to get $y^2 = 81^2$.

Before we find the value of 81^2, note that the question asks for the value of $y^2 - \sqrt{y}$, which means we'll have to square 81 and then subtract 9. If we square 81, the last digit will end in a "1" (because when you multiply 81 by 81, the last digit will be 1 × 1 = 1). Then, when we subtract 9, the last digit will have to be 11 − 9 = 2. There's only one answer that ends in a "2," choice (D). Here's a demonstration. We know that $y^2 = 81^2 = 81 \times 81 = 6,561$ (ends in a "1"). Now, we need to subtract 9 because we want the value of $y^2 - \sqrt{y}$ and $\sqrt{y} = 9$. So, $6,561 - 9 = 6,552$ (ends in a "2").

19. The correct answer is (E). $1 + q^3$

This problem required us to see that one of the terms is a q, not a p like the others. Then, because we are not given the value of q, our answer choice must have a q-term in it. We can zap choice (A) right away. Then, let's plug in the value of (-1) for p. Then, we get:

$$p + p^2 + p^4 + q^3 = (-1) + (-1)^2 + (-1)^4 + q^3$$
$$= -1 + 1 + 1 + q^3$$
$$= 1 + q^3, \text{ which is choice (E).}$$

20. The correct answer is (C). 5

We were told in high school to cross-multiply and solve for x. But here's a much faster method. Start from the choices and plug in values for x.

Remember, when plugging in values, we want to always start from choice (C). So, let's plug in values for $x = 5$.

Then, we get $\dfrac{5+3}{6} = \dfrac{12}{5+4}$

That is, $\dfrac{8}{6} = \dfrac{12}{9}$. Cross-multiplying, we get $72 = 72$

Hey, it works. So stop here. Of course, you can always cross-multiply and solve as presented. But we think plugging in values is faster.

21. The correct answer is (D). 496

From the graph, we see that 16% of the students in JFK School are in 5th grade and 15% are in 6th grade. Thus, the total percent of students in JFK School who are in 5th and 6th grades is 15% + 16% = 31%.

We know that there are 1,600 students in JFK School. So, the total number of students in 5th and 6th grades is:

31% of 1,600 = .31 × 1,600 = 496.

22. The correct answer is (B). 2

From the graph, we see that 10% of the students in Lincoln School are in 4th grade. There are a total of 2,400 students in Lincoln School. This means that the number of students in 4th grade is 10% of 2,400 = .10 × 2,400 = 240.

Now we need to find out how many grades in JFK School have 240 or more students. The fastest way to find this is to look at the total enrollment in JFK School and see what percent constitutes 240 students. Because there are 1,600 students in JFK School, we know that 10% of that would be 160. We need 80 more to get 240. If 10% is 160, then 5% must be 80. Now we see that 160 and 80 make 240, which means that we're looking for 15% or higher in JFK School. We see that grades 5 and 6 have 15% or more, which means that the number of grades with 240 or more students is 2.

23. The correct answer is (E). 1,008

We need to know the number of students in Lincoln School's 6th, 7th, and 8th grades. First, let's add up the percentages in these three grades: 14% + 15% + 13% = 42%. We know that there are 2,400 students in that school. So now we need to find 42% of 2,400.

We know that 10% of 2,400 = 240. This means 40% is four times as much, or 240 × 4 = 960. We now need to find 2% more. But first, look at your answers. Only one answer, choice (E), 1,008, is more than 960, which means that has to be the right answer. No need to go further.

24. The correct answer is (C). 20.00

We know that 15% of all students in JFK are in 6th grade. This is .15 × 1,600 = 240 students. If 100 more students get enrolled in 6th grade, the total number of students in 6th grade is 240 + 100 = 340.

But notice that when 100 more students get enrolled, the total enrollment of the school also goes up by 100. So the new enrollment is 1,600 + 100 = 1,700.

We now need to know what percent of 1,700 is 340. We know that 10% of 1,700 is 170, and so 20% is double that, which is 340. In other words 20% of all students are 6th graders.

25. The correct answer is (C). 9

At present, JFK School's enrollment is 1,600 out of 4,000, or 40%. With the additions, JFK School's enrollment is 2,000 out of a total of 4,500, or 44.4%. So, the change is from 40 to 44, or 4 percent. To find percent increase, use the following formula:

$$\text{percent change} = \frac{\text{change}}{\text{starting point}} \times 100$$

$$= \frac{4}{44.4} \times 100 = \frac{1}{11.1} \times 100 \approx 9\%$$

26. The correct answer is (B). 625

We recall that an *odd* digit is one that is not a multiple of 2. So the question is asking: How many four-digit numbers can we make using just the numbers 1, 3, 5, 7, and 9? To make a number, there are four digits that we have to fill, and there are five choices for what number to put in each position.

To calculate the total number of possible choices, we *multiply* the number of choices that we have for each position together—in this case, $5 \times 5 \times 5 \times 5 = 5^4 = 625$ (if we could use *even* digits too, this number would be 10^4, or 10,000). Notice, you don't actually have to multiply this number. Once you figured out that it was $5 \times 5 \times 5 \times 5$, you could tell that the answer has to be choice (B). Why? Because that's the only answer that ends in a 5.

27. The correct answer is (B). –1

To find an expression for $\{n + 1\}$, we apply the definition of the $\{\}$ operator:

$$\{m\} = m\,(1 - m)$$

To find $\{n + 1\}$, rewrite this equation and put "$n + 1$" everywhere that an "m" appears:

$$\{n + 1\} = (n + 1)\,(1 - [n + 1])$$
$$= (n + 1)\,(1 - n - 1)$$
$$= (n + 1)\,(-n)$$
$$= -n^2 - n.$$

So to solve the problem $n + 1 = \{n + 1\}$, we will want to solve the equation

$$n + 1 = -n^2 - n.$$

If we add $n^2 + n$ to both sides of this equation, we get

$$n^2 + 2n + 1 = 0$$

We recognize the left side of this expression as $(n + 1)^2$ and conclude that this equation is true only if $n = -1$, choice (B).

28. The correct answer is (C). $\dfrac{25}{2\sqrt{2}}$

First, let's note that the radius of the semicircle is 5. We know this because the coordinates of B are $(5,0)$, which means radius OB is 5. To find the area of the triangle, we need its base and its height. We can take $\overline{OC}$ as the base. We know that $\overline{OC}$ is also the radius of the semicircle, which has measure 5. So, the base of the triangle is 5. We now need its height.

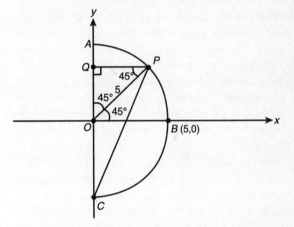

If we use $\overline{OC}$ as the base, we need a perpendicular from $\overline{OC}$ (or from an extension of $\overline{OC}$) to the opposite corner. To find this perpendicular, let's draw $\overline{PQ}$, perpendicular to $\overline{OA}$. Then, $\overline{PQ}$ is the height of the triangle. We need to find PQ.

Because m$\angle POB$ is 45 degrees, m$\angle POQ$ is also 45 degrees (because the two 45-degree angles form the 90-degree angle between the x- and y-axes). If m$\angle POQ$ is 45 and m$\angle PQO$ is 90, then m$\angle OPQ$ must also be 45 degrees so that the three angles sum to 180 degrees. So, triangle PQO is a 45-45-90 triangle. Notice also that $\overline{OP}$ is another radius, which means OP is 5.

We know that in a 45-45-90 triangle, the hypotenuse is $\sqrt{2}$ times each perpendicular side. In other words, the hypotenuse, 5, is $\sqrt{2}$ times the height PQ. So, $5 = \sqrt{2}\,(PQ)$.

And, $\quad\quad\quad \dfrac{5}{\sqrt{2}} = PQ$.

So, now we have base = 5 and height =

$$\frac{5}{\sqrt{2}}$$

Then, area of triangle $OPC = \frac{1}{2} \times 5 \times \frac{5}{\sqrt{2}}$

$$= \frac{25}{2\sqrt{2}}$$

29. The correct answer is (C). 7

We know that the total sum of all the cards in each box must be equal to 18. Box A has two cards that are already determined for us. Two of the cards are 6's. Therefore, the sum of the two cards in box A is 12. Thus, the other four cards must sum to 6. Each card is numbered 1 through 6. We want three of the four cards to be as small as possible. Therefore, the three cards should be 1's. This leaves us with the fourth card as 3.

Sum of cards in box A: 6 + 6 + 1 + 1 + 1 + 3 = 18.

For box B, two of the cards are 5's. This leaves us with four cards. Again, we want three of the four cards to be as small as possible. Let the three cards be 1's. This leaves the fourth card as 5. But recall that neither card was a 5 or a 6. Thus, the fourth card must be smaller than 5. We see that if the fourth card is 4 and one of the other cards is 2, we have:

Sum of cards in box B: 5 + 5 + 1 + 1 + 2 + 4 = 18.

So, the largest possible sum of the two cards is 3 + 4 = 7.

30. The correct answer is (A). p × d

There are a number of ways of working this problem. But first, let's make use of the given information to write an equation. We are told that the ratio of the perimeter of the larger to the smaller rectangle is p. That is,

$$\frac{\text{perimeter of larger rectangle}}{\text{perimeter of smaller rectangle}} = p$$

In terms of length and width, we know that the perimeter is $2(L + B)$ for the larger rectangle and $2(l + b)$ for the smaller rectangle. Then the ratio of the two perimeters is

$$\frac{2(L+B)}{2(l+b)} = p,$$ which can be simplified to

$$\frac{(L+B)}{(l+b)} = p.$$ Call this Equation (1).

We are also told that $\frac{(L-B)}{(l-b)} = d.$ Call this Equation (2). Now multiply Equation (1) and Equation (2) so that we get

$$\frac{(L+B)}{(l+b)} \times \frac{(L-B)}{(l-b)} = p \times d$$

Ah, both the numerator and the denominator are of the form $(a + b) \times (a - b)$ and are equal to $(a^2 - b^2)$.

Using the same formula, we multiply the numerators together and the denominators together to get

$$\frac{(L^2 - B^2)}{(l^2 - b^2)} = p \times d,$$ which is choice (A).

Don't be surprised that this was a difficult problem. It appears near the end of the exam; it is meant to be difficult.

But, let's see if there is an easier way to do the problem. If you don't like to deal with variables like p and d, give values to L, B, l, and b. To make calculations easy, let $L = 4$, $B = 2$, $l = 2$, and $b = 1$. Then, the ratio of the two perimeters is given by:

$$\frac{(L+L+B+B)}{(l+l+b+b)} = \frac{(4+4+2+2)}{(2+2+1+1)} = \frac{12}{6} = p = 2$$

Similarly, $\frac{(L-B)}{(l-b)} = \frac{(4-2)}{(2-1)} = \frac{2}{1} = d = 2$

We are asked to find $\left(\frac{L^2 - B^2}{l^2 - b^2} \right)$. Substituting our own values, we get

$$\frac{4^2 - 2^2}{2^2 - 1^2} = \frac{16-4}{3} = \frac{12}{3} = 4$$

Now look at the answer choices. Choice (A) is p × d, which is equal to 2 × 2 = 4. As you can see, choice (A) gives us the required value, and so it is the right answer. At this point, we don't need to try the other choices.

Day 11

Test 1, Part 2: Verbal (1).

Questions and Answers

Assignment for Today:

Take the first part of a practice GRE Verbal Test under actual test conditions. Allow yourself exactly 30 minutes to complete the 38 questions in this test.

Directions: *For questions 1–7, one or more words have been left out of each sentence. Circle the answer, A–E, that contains the word or words that best fit the meaning of the entire sentence.*

---

1. The food server admitted that her work was just a job and that she was doing it for the sake of _____ and nothing else.

   (A) approbation

   (B) remuneration

   (C) emulation

   (D) exoneration

   (E) procrastination

2. According to the minority political party, the major problem with national health insurance reform, as a _____ alternative to more government spending, is that it's a tax _____.

   (A) purported..increase

   (B) cheery..standard

   (C) feasible..revolt

   (D) sarcastic..statement

   (E) toxic..shelter

3. Because the bulk of tax revenue comes from various sales taxes, the burden of payment falls _____ on the shoulders of poor and middle-income Americans who spend roughly 16 percent of their incomes on taxable goods, while the richest Americans spend only about 3.1 percent.

   (A) disproportionately

   (B) diminutively

   (C) lightly

   (D) inadequately

   (E) equitably

4. After the wind blew away the musician's music, she _____ so cleverly that the people watching were not _____ of the mishap.

   (A) extemporized..cognizant

   (B) digressed..unappreciative

   (C) improvised..warned

   (D) wafted..aware

   (E) denigrated..mindful

5. The dermatologist was ____ that the new surgical procedure he worked ten years to invent would be able to ____ all signs of having a tattoo.

   (A) unwavering..expunge

   (B) incredulous..erase

   (C) sentient..obliterate

   (D) timorous..eradicate

   (E) euphoric..exacerbate

6. When the mayor announced her candidacy for the next term, she ____ the virtues of her past term while the reporters took copious notes and wished she weren't so ____.

   (A) explained..taciturn

   (B) expatiated on..garrulous

   (C) expounded on..insidious

   (D) gibbered about..erudite

   (E) noted..talkative

7. After work, Miriam would go home and enjoy ____ with her husband and children, but at work, she talked in lofty tones that were reminiscent of a ____.

   (A) bantering..colloquy

   (B) housework..discourse

   (C) discussion..eulogy

   (D) hoopla..secretary

   (E) quibbling..scholar

Directions: *For questions 8–16, determine the relationship between the two words given in capital letters. Then, from the choices listed A–E, select the one pair that has a relationship most similar to that of the capitalized pair. Circle the letter of that pair.*

---

8. STATESMAN:GOVERNMENT::

   (A) teacher:faculty

   (B) potter:art

   (C) raconteur:anecdote

   (D) dowager:marriage

   (E) shepherd:farm

9. COBBLER:OXFORDS::

   (A) mason:mortar

   (B) lapidary:stones

   (C) haberdasher:linen

   (D) chandler:candles

   (E) agronomist:fertilizer

10. RIB:THORAX::

    (A) tibia:fibula

    (B) tendon:muscle

    (C) pennant:flagpole

    (D) odometer:dashboard

    (E) grass:sidewalk

11. SURREPTITIOUS:CANDOR::

    (A) stealthy:mystery

    (B) confident:honesty

    (C) fearless:pride

    (D) fatuous:sense

    (E) subtle:cunning

12. PAGE:TOME::

    (A) ink:paper

    (B) tree:forest

    (C) rose:petal

    (D) sky:sun

    (E) thespian:stage

13. RAINBOW:EPHEMERAL::

    (A) dolt:sagacious

    (B) fanatic:zealous

    (C) dinosaur:complacent

    (D) connoisseur:stoic

    (E) ocean:static

14. FORUM:DISCUSSION::

    (A) papacy:absolution

    (B) space:exploration

    (C) parliament:legislation

    (D) rostrum:peroration

    (E) speakeasy:gossip

15. EXCORIATE:ABRADE::

   (A) consent:decree

   (B) demur:agree

   (C) mar:burnish

   (D) eschew:avoid

   (E) proscribe:support

16. MNEMONIC:REMEMBER::

   (A) amnesiac:forget

   (B) euphoria:relax

   (C) nostril:smell

   (D) audio:hear

   (E) glasses:see

Directions: *Read each passage and answer the questions that follow. Base your answers only on what is stated or implied in the passage. Circle the letter of your answer choice.*

Questions 17–24 are based on the following passage.

Before I became law editor for a farm paper, I used to doubt the genuineness of some of the absurd queries one occasionally sees propounded in the "Answers to Correspondents"
(5) columns of newspapers. Now I am almost prepared to believe that a Utah man actually wrote Bill Nye for information concerning the nature and habits of Limburg cheese, as a basis for experiments in the use of that substance as motive
(10) power.

Of the hundreds of queries that come to my office in the course of a year, most of them are commonplace enough, including such questions as what constitutes a lawful fence in Connecti-
(15) cut. But one correspondent in 50 unconsciously sends in a gem that gives the editor a smile with which to rest his tired countenance, albeit there is often concomitant pathos in the letters.

Many a pathetic domestic snarl is disclosed in
(20) amusing language. For instance, one woman wrote, "My husband's health is very poor and he is stubborn about making a will." She sought advice concerning her property rights, contingent

upon her spouse's "stubbornness" remaining
(25) with him to the end.

Sometimes the wife holds the upper hand, as illustrated by a Wisconsin farmer who complained: "Came to Wis., bought 160 A, put it in my Wife's name, and as soon as she found out
(30) that the law of Wis. gave the husband absolutely nothing, she will not give me *one cent*, or go a single place, or will not buy me any clothe, only working clothe. Now, can I compel her to pay me a salary, without leaving her. And I shopped
(35) three horses, one cow, one calf, one brood sow, wagon and harness, buggy and harness, and can *I* dispose of them?" This Mr. Bumble was told that he was at liberty to "go places" as he saw fit, could control the stock enumerated, and dic-
(40) tate the terms on which he would work in his wife's vineyard, but that the Wisconsin law makes her secure in the sole ownership of the farm which he unadvisedly caused to be conveyed to her.

(45) Another rebellious husband writes that he conveyed his property to his wife to defeat his judgment creditors. "Now I want my wife to Deed some of it back to me but she refuses to do that on account the feeling is not at best between
(50) us." He wanted to know if it wouldn't be a good plan to confess to the creditors, and get the property deeded "back to me as it was before as the hole Deal was a Fraud." The main objection to this plan being that it would enable the creditors
(55) to get the property, it was suggested that Friend Wife be permitted to retain control, especially since he could not compel her to revest title in him.

Another case is stated as follows: "The con-
(60) tents of case are—A newly married couple, the young lady having come to the decision that life is unbearable to live with her husband because she hates him and cannot bear his ways of manners. She wishes them to part, and he will not
(65) agree to it. And she thinks of going to her parents to live, and take her belongings that she had before being married with him, and the husband says no—what has she a right to do? Or does the belongings belong to him also?" Without

(70) encouragement to a domestic rupture, the correspondent was told that a woman's ownership of personal property is not affected by her marriage.

A jilted girl sought advice about how to "fix" her unfaithful sweetheart. He promised marriage (75) three times, but as the wedding day approached he "always had some excuse. If it weren't the crops, it was the widow-women. If it weren't the widow-women, it was something else. He never had written his love for me in a letter. But when (80) I was with him he was all love and kisses and so on. He said in one of his letters, 'Make all you can this fall in no matter what kind of work as it may not last forever.' But he has backed out now for good."

(85)   But problems of the heart are by no means the only cause for correspondence. Rights between employer and employee are frequently called into question. One indignant woman employed on a farm objected that the "landlord brought out (90) a large worthless dog and we have been feeding him, have been paying thirty dollars a sack for flour and twenty-two dollars per week for corn meal to feed him. We have asked several times to take him away as we cannot afford to feed (95) him. This mutt is no earthly account for any thing and he seldom gets up. He just lies there, wagging his tail, eager for his meals. We don't need or want him here and have told him so."

I disclaim any intention to unduly discredit (100) the intelligence or high-mindedness of any of my correspondents for, as already intimated, the freak letters are few as compared with the general run of submissions. My observations in reading thousands confirm my belief that most (105) people, regardless of their wealth or walk in life, stand upon an equal plane intellectually and morally, when fair allowance is made of individual opportunities and environment. I may smile for a moment or two over the occasional (110) rude spelling or unschooled language of one writer out of 50, but I sober up when I reflect that he or she may have earned a larger percentage of dividend on the opportunities presented than I have on mine.

17. The main purpose of this passage most likely is to
    (A) examine the different types of commonly occurring domestic disputes.
    (B) describe the failed schemes of people who try to outwit the law.
    (C) analyze the legal recourse available to people in oppressive situations.
    (D) determine the role of a newspaper in helping its readers through advice columns.
    (E) validate the authenticity of strange but heartfelt submissions that newspapers publish.

18. The word "conveyed" in line 44 most likely means
    (A) trusted.
    (B) transported.
    (C) transferred.
    (D) bequeathed.
    (E) bypassed.

19. The author probably wades through submissions to the paper with
    (A) incessant laughter.
    (B) weary disillusionment.
    (C) restrained contempt.
    (D) profound disbelief.
    (E) infrequent smiles.

20. The author relates the story of Mr. Bumble the farmer in order to
    (A) warn farmers that Wisconsin law can be dangerous.
    (B) emphasize that some wives are suffering in silence while waiting for a chance to gain the upper hand.
    (C) highlight a turning point in the forces that brought about the liberation of women.
    (D) illustrate the pitfalls of not taking legal advice before trusting someone even as close as a wife.
    (E) to entertain the reader with a pathetic but amusingly worded domestic dispute.

21. The essential difference between the Limburg cheese letter and the letter in paragraph three is that the Limburg cheese letter was

(A) a freak letter whereas the other letter was commonplace.

(B) merely absurd whereas the other letter was amusing.

(C) written by a Utah man and the other letter by a Connecticut woman.

(D) an information query while the other letter was for legal advocacy.

(E) concerned with powerful odors and the other letter with stubbornness.

22. In this passage, the author probably uses excerpts from submissions

(A) so readers may judge for themselves the extent to which farming communities are petty and illiterate.

(B) because they possess an amusing flavor that is lost if converted to polished prose.

(C) to lend authenticity to what might otherwise be unconvincing narrative.

(D) to show that pathetic snarls can have an amusing facet if only linguistically.

(E) so the reader may not misinterpret the information or suspect the author of fabrication.

23. From the various examples used in the passage, the reader can conclude that

(A) the farm paper is based in Utah or Wisconsin.

(B) Wisconsin law stipulates that in a farm, the wife secures sole ownership.

(C) hating your husband's unbearable manners is sufficient grounds for divorce.

(D) large dogs are capable of consuming 62 dollars' worth of meal in a week.

(E) some farm people were not hesitant to solicit advice from newspapers.

24. Which of the following can be inferred from the advocacy given in one or more of the cases mentioned?

(A) The farm and livestock do belong to his wife, but Mr. Bumble may decide how he wants to work on it.

(B) If a deal was based on fraud, it can be rendered null and void.

(C) A wife retains control over her personal property even if her husband raises a dispute.

(D) A general statement in a letter is not legally considered as a sign of intent to marry.

(E) A landlord has the right to add livestock or animals to a farm without the tenant's consent.

Questions 25–27 are based on the following passage.

One of the strangest facts in literary criticism is that, after more than 40 years of intense and occasionally even feverish activity on the part of scholars of Beckman, the question of what is

(5) Beckman's "Song to Me" is still a legitimate one. If the poem were a brief and much-mutilated fragment containing part of a single episode, the present state of criticism would be understandable and excusable. But of this poem we have

(10) nearly all that was written or planned by the author. Though incomplete, the extant copy contains 21,258 lines, and it obviously can never have been intended to contain much more. We have, therefore, in the present version, nearly all

(15) that he intended to write.

Moreover, we have, as an indication of the meaning of the poem, the title given by the author himself. And we have a positive and definite statement not only of the main features of

(20) the narrative as far as it is preserved to us but also of the principal incident of the unwritten portion.

Why, then, are not the purpose and meaning of the poem clear and well recognized? Several

(25) reasons may be suggested.

In the first place, much of the study devoted to this poem has been concerned not with the interpretation of the author's meaning but with the discovery of the sources of his materials. What
(30) suggested the temple? And the figures on the walls? And the treeless desert? Did the eagle come from Ovid, or from Dante, or from folklore? Whence came the ice-capped mountain and the revolving house? Correct answers to these ques-
(35) tions would be interesting. If rightly used, they might be important. But they could hardly, in any event, contribute largely to the interpretation of the poem, for an author's meaning depends not upon where he got his material, but upon what
(40) use he makes of it.

That students of Beckman should persist in interpreting him allegorically is strange. As a matter of fact, his work is singularly free from allegory in the strict sense of the term. The mere
(45) presence of nonhuman actors, whether animal or mythological or even personified abstractions, does not create allegory. For this, there must be symbolism of action or of character. But a debate between two girls concerning their lover is not
(50) allegory, even if birds take sides and debate and fight, and the decision is left to the god of love or his representative.

25. According to the passage, Beckman scholars benefit from all of the following EXCEPT

(A) the extant copy of the poem has 21,258 lines.

(B) "Song of Me" has always been published as the author intended.

(C) Beckman himself gave the work a title.

(D) the principal incident surrounding the poem is clear.

(E) the present version of the poem is faithful to Beckman's intention.

26. The author of the passage implies that an allegorical reading of Beckman's work is "strange" because

(A) allegories are common in the Bible, and Beckman was not religious when he wrote this poem.

(B) the poem lacks personified abstractions.

(C) "Song to Me" does not suggest that the plot or the characters are symbolic of anything.

(D) Beckman used other works to explore allegory.

(E) birds and other animals are the actors instead of people.

27. According to the passage, in order to understand "Song to Me" more fully, scholars should

(A) examine the competing editions of the text to see what Beckman's intended meaning was.

(B) discover the sources for the elements of Beckman's work.

(C) view the poem as an extended allegory of opposing forces.

(D) abandon current lines of scholarship and further explore basic questions about meaning and purpose.

(E) balance their research between criticism and interpretation.

Directions: *For questions 28–38, select the lettered choice most nearly opposite in meaning to the word given in CAPITAL letters. Circle the letter of your choice.*

---

28. UNANIMOUS:

(A) luminous

(B) agreeable

(C) discordant

(D) united

(E) uniform

29. DELINQUENT:
   (A) juvenile
   (B) mischievous
   (C) delayed
   (D) early
   (E) delicate

30. ROTUND:
   (A) angular
   (B) tall
   (C) stout
   (D) straight
   (E) dietetic

31. FORTHRIGHT:
   (A) furthermost
   (B) fatuous
   (C) fatalistic
   (D) furtive
   (E) fortuitous

32. LATENT:
   (A) dormant
   (B) rubber
   (C) patent
   (D) plastic
   (E) paternal

33. GALE:
   (A) storm
   (B) breeze
   (C) monsoon
   (D) anemometer
   (E) blizzard

34. MELLIFLUOUS:
   (A) melodious
   (B) superfluous
   (C) grating
   (D) superficial
   (E) melancholy

35. WAX:
   (A) melt
   (B) wave
   (C) dull
   (D) shine
   (E) wane

36. FALLACIOUS:
   (A) irrational
   (B) valid
   (C) indifferent
   (D) faulty
   (E) logical

37. PERVIOUS:
   (A) permeable
   (B) previous
   (C) pernicious
   (D) prescient
   (E) impenetrable

38. ORBICULAR:
   (A) round
   (B) convoluted
   (C) planetary
   (D) straight
   (E) visionary

Quick Answer Guide

Test 1, Part 2: Verbal (1)

1. B	11. D	21. D	31. D
2. A	12. B	22. C	32. C
3. A	13. B	23. E	33. B
4. A	14. C	24. C	34. C
5. A	15. D	25. B	35. E
6. B	16. E	26. C	36. B
7. A	17. E	27. D	37. E
8. C	18. C	28. C	38. D
9. D	19. E	29. D	
10. D	20. E	30. A	

For explanations to these questions, see Day 12.

Test 1, Part 2: Verbal (1).

Explanations and Strategies

Assignment for Today:

Review the explanations for the Verbal Test you took on Day 11.

1. The correct answer is (B). remuneration

The sentence makes it pretty clear that the server is working just for the money. So to find the right answer, select the word that has something to do with earning money. Choice (B) fits just right. *Remuneration* means compensation or money.

The food server said her work was just a job and that she was doing it for the *remuneration* and nothing else.

2. The correct answer is (A). purported..increase

You can find the right answer to this question by using a different strategy for each blank. First, think of what word you might use for the second blank. The sentence should tell you that having national health care is going to raise taxes. Choice (A) fits beautifully here. Now try the elimination strategy for the first blank. Again, nothing works very well here except *purported* in choice (A).

According to the minority political party, the major problem with national health insurance reform, as a *purported* alternative to more government spending, is that it's a tax *increase*.

3. The correct answer is (A). disproportionately

Note the flag word, "because," at the beginning of the sentence. This tells you that the last part of the sentence is caused by the first part.

The sentence tells us that the tax burden is nearly five times greater for poor and middle-income Americans than for rich Americans. In other words, the tax load is lopsided. An adverb that means uneven or inequitable would fit the context nicely. So choice (A), *disproportionately*—which means unevenly distributed—is the correct answer.

Because the bulk of tax revenue comes from various sales taxes, the burden of payment falls *disproportionately* on the shoulders of poor and middle-income Americans who spend roughly 16 percent of their incomes on taxable goods, while the richest Americans spend only about 3.1 percent.

4. The correct answer is (A). extemporized..cognizant

The sentence itself gives you some major clues even before you see the possible choices. First off, if a musician loses her music, she will either have to stop playing or make stuff up as she goes along. The sentence indicates that the musician is clever, so you can be fairly sure she made stuff up. The people watching did not notice what she did. So look for words that fit these ideas. Choice (A) works best.

After the wind blew away the musician's music, she *extemporized* so cleverly that the people watching were not *cognizant* of the mishap.

5. The correct answer is (A). unwavering..expunge

The easy part about this question is deciding what kinds of words will adequately fill the blanks— something like "hopeful" and "erase." The hard part is knowing which words have these meanings. Choice (A) offers *unwavering*, which means solidly confident, and *expunge*, which means to remove all evidence of existence. This is the best choice.

The dermatologist was *unwavering* that the new surgical procedure he worked ten years to invent would be able to *expunge* all signs of having a tattoo.

6. The correct answer is (B). expatiated on..garrulous

The best bet for finding the correct choice is to simply read in the choices, eliminating those that don't work well. Then you will have to make some fine distinctions about which choice best fits the context of the sentence. All in all, choice (B) works best. To *expatiate* is to elaborate. This works well for a politician. *Garrulous* means talkative—another good word for a politician.

When the mayor announced her candidacy for the next term, she *expatiated on* the virtues of her past term while the reporters took copious notes and wished she weren't so *garrulous*.

7. The correct answer is (A). bantering..colloquy

The sentence clues and the flag word "but" indicate that the first blank is best filled by a word that means "light talk," while the second word should mean "serious talk." Choice (A) fits the best here. *Bantering* means playful kidding. A *colloquy*, in contrast, is a serious conference.

After work, Miriam would go home and enjoy *bantering* with her husband and children, but at work, she talked in lofty tones that were reminiscent of a *colloquy*.

8. The correct answer is (C). raconteur:anecdote

statesman—a person skilled in the art of government.
government—the control of the actions of a community or nation.

A *statesman* is a person skilled in the art of *government*.

Is a *raconteur* skilled in the art of *anecdote*? Yes. A *raconteur* is a person skilled in relating *anecdotes* interestingly (an expert teller).

9. The correct answer is (D). chandler:candles

cobbler—a person who makes shoes.
oxfords—shoes, something worn on the foot.

A *cobbler* makes *oxfords*.

Does a *chandler* make *candles*? Yes! A *chandler* is a *candle* maker. Therefore, *cobbler* is to *oxfords* as *chandler* is to *candles*.

10. The correct answer is (D). odometer:dashboard

rib—one of the 24 bones that cover the thorax.
thorax—the front part of the body, between the neck and the belly; the chest.

A *rib* is part of the *thorax*.

Is an *odometer* part of the *dashboard*? Yes. An *odometer* is an instrument that shows the number of miles traveled and is part of the *dashboard* in an automobile.

11. The correct answer is (D). fatuous:sense

surreptitious—to be secretive.
candor—honesty and sincerity.

To be *surreptitious* means to lack *candor*.

Does being *fatuous* mean to lack *sense*? Yes. To be *fatuous* is to be silly and inane.

12. The correct answer is (B). tree:forest

page—a single sheet of paper in a book.
tome—a large or scholarly book.

A *tome* consists of many *pages*.

Does a *forest* consist of many *trees*? Yes. Therefore, a *tome* consists of many *pages* in the same way that a *forest* consists of many *trees*.

13. The correct answer is (B). fanatic:zealous

ephemeral—lasting a very short time.
rainbow—a short-lived phenomenon in the sky.

A characteristic of a *rainbow* is that it is *ephemeral*.

Is a *fanatic zealous*? Yes! A *fanatic* is one who exhibits intense devotion or *zeal*. Therefore, *rainbow* is to *ephemeral* as *fanatic* is to *zealous*.

14. The correct answer is (C). parliament:legislation

forum—an assembly for the discussion of public affairs.
discussion—debate, exchange of views, examination by argument.

A *forum* is a body of people assembled for *discussion*.

Is a *parliament* a body assembled for *legislation*? Yes. *Parliament* is the *legislative* body of representatives that makes or enacts laws.

15. The correct answer is (D). eschew:avoid

excoriate—to wear off the skin.
abrade—to rub away by friction.

To *excoriate* is the same as to *abrade*.

Is to *eschew* the same as to *avoid*? Yes.

16. The correct answer is (E). glasses:see

mnemonic—a device used to aid memory.
remember—to recall.

A *mnemonic* is a device used to help one *remember*.

Are *glasses* a device used to help one *see*? *Glasses* are a device used to correct poor vision, thus enabling a person to *see* more clearly.

17. The correct answer is (E).

This passage seems to contain a series of anecdotes or different incidents. In this case, the first paragraph contains clues that tie them together.

In the first sentence, the author admits he used to question the validity or genuineness of submissions in newspaper columns. The author then lists a number of strange cases he received, news of which convinced him that unusual submissions were authentic.

18. The correct answer is (C).

"Convey" can mean "transport, transmit, communicate" or, in a legal context, "transfer" (titles, deeds, property, etc.). The context here is legal. Besides, none of the other choices makes sense when you talk about property, such as a farm.

19. The correct answer is (E).

Lines 15–17 tell us that "one correspondent in 50 unconsciously sends in a gem that gives the editor a smile with which to rest his tired countenance." This implies that 49 out of 50 submissions don't make the editor smile. "Infrequent (or occasional) smiles" describes this nicely. The other choices don't come close.

20. The correct answer is (E).

The author is trying to tell the reader that advice columns describe real problems or situations, even if they seem funny or strange. Given this purpose, only choice (E) makes sense. The other choices assume that the author is trying to give advice.

21. The correct answer is (D).

This choice sounds too superficial or easy. But all the other choices have something wrong with them. We know the former was written for "information concerning the nature and habits of Limburg cheese" (lines 7–8). We know the latter was for "advice concerning her property rights" (line 23). That's enough evidence to support this choice.

22. The correct answer is (C).

What sounds like a personal judgment really has to do with the author's main purpose in the passage. The author is out to entertain readers and convince them that advice columns are not made up. Keeping this in mind, it becomes obvious that choice (C) is the best answer. One good way of supporting the authenticity of a column and making it more believable is to have different submissions, each with its own characteristics.

23. The correct answer is (E).

This looks like a simple choice. It doesn't say much. But the other choices can be ruled out because of obvious inaccuracies. The passage speaks of farm people who asked for advice. Logical inference: Some farm people were not hesitant to solicit advice from newspapers.

24. The correct answer is (C).

The question is very specific. Which of the following can be inferred from the *advocacy* given, *not* from the descriptions or disputes? Examine each choice carefully against the passage. In lines 70–72, " . . . the correspondent was told that a woman's ownership of personal property is not affected by her marriage." So a wife's dispute with her husband cannot affect personal property.

25. The correct answer is (B).

According to the passage, all the statements given are helpful to Beckman scholars except choice (B). The passage says nothing about the publication history of the poem. Furthermore, the publication history would be less beneficial to these specific scholars than the other facts, which deal with Beckman's idea about what the poem should be and mean.

26. The correct answer is (C).

In order to have allegory, the author states, "there must be symbolism of action or of character." Because the author argues against reading "Song of Me" as an allegory, we can safely conclude that the poem does not suggest this kind of symbolism.

27. The correct answer is (D).

It should be clear that the author wants scholars to get away from two current lines of research: sources of materials and allegorical criticism. In many ways, the author is asking his colleagues to get back to the basic questions of purpose and meaning without wandering off into more alluring (and, to him, less productive) scholarship. The author here is still eager to see great scholarship done on meaning and purpose.

28. The correct answer is (C). discordant

Unanimous means in complete agreement.

Discordant means in disagreement, clashing, conflicting. It's the opposite of *unanimous*.

29. The correct answer is (D). early

Delinquent means late, failing in duty, or unpaid.

Early means premature or before its time. Is *early* the opposite of *delinquent*? As *delinquent* can mean late (such as "your payment is delinquent"), this is a good choice.

30. The correct answer is (A). angular

Rotund means rounded or chubby.

Angular means lean or sharp-edged. Is *angular* the opposite of *rotund*? Yes.

31. The correct answer is (D). furtive

Forthright means straight to the point.

Furtive means sneaky, surreptitious. Is *furtive* the opposite of *forthright*? Yes, to be indirect (*furtive*) is the opposite of straight to the point (*forthright*).

32. The correct answer is (C). patent

Latent means potential, concealed or hidden.

Patent means obvious or exposed (among other meanings). It's nearly opposite of *latent*.

33. The correct answer is (B). breeze

Gale means a very strong wind.

Breeze means a light wind. Is a *breeze* the opposite of a *gale*? Yes—a *breeze* is a light wind, whereas a *gale* is a strong wind.

34. The correct answer is (C). grating

Mellifluous means smooth or pleasant sounding.

   Grating means hard, unpleasant. Is *grating* the opposite of *mellifluous*? Yes—sweet musical sounds would be *mellifluous*, not *grating*.

35. The correct answer is (E). wane

Wax means grow larger.

   Wane means grow smaller in size. Is *wane* the opposite of *wax*? Yes, *wax* means grow larger in size.

36. The correct answer is (B). valid

Fallacious means faulty, false, or negative.

   Valid means sound, true, or reasonable. Is *valid* the opposite of *fallacious*? Yes, the two words provide you with several excellent opposite meanings.

37. The correct answer is (E). impenetrable

Pervious means penetrable.

   Impenetrable means impervious. Is *impenetrable* the opposite of *pervious*? Yes.

38. The correct answer is (D). straight

Orbicular means round, bulb-shaped.

   Straight means shallow. Is *straight* the opposite of *orbicular*? Yes, planets move in round—not straight—orbits.

Test 1, Part 3A: Issue Essay

Sample Topic

Assignment for Today:

Write an issue essay on the given topic. Time limit: 45 minutes.

For the following exercise, we recommend that you set aside 45 minutes of uninterrupted time. Clear your desk, except for some scratch paper and a stop watch, and take this test under real test-like conditions.

Present your perspective on the issue below, using relevant reasons and/or examples to support your views.

"Who we are depends far more on situational factors, such as our environment and our social context, than on our personality."

Before you write your essay, follow the steps outlined in the strategy section.

<u>Your position</u> (underline one or more):

		Qualified	Question
Support	Oppose	support	assumption

Now write down points that you will make.

1. _____

2. _____

3. _____

4. _____

5. _____

Next, renumber the points above so that you begin and end with your strongest ones. After you feel comfortable with the sequence, begin writing your issue essay. On Day 14, you will see how we have approached the task.

Test 1, Part 3A: Issue Essay

Sample Essay Response

Assignment for Today:

Analyze your issue essay from Day 13.

NOTES FOR SAMPLE RESPONSE

"Who we are depends far more on situational factors, such as our environment and our social context, than on our personality."

<u>Your position</u> (underline one or more):

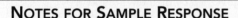

		Qualified	Question
<u>Support</u>	Oppose	support	assumption

As you can see, we have decided to support the position that who we are depends on situational factors more than on personality.

Here is a sample of points that one might make:

1. If false, we would have the same attitude in all environments.

2. I hold different attitudes in different contexts.

3. Example of one attitude

4. Example of another attitude

5. Can we really know what "personality" is?

The best way to know how you did on your essay is to have someone else read it for clarity, grammar, and substance. If you have friends, teachers, or family members who are willing to read your paper, take advantage of their input. They can see holes in your arguments and comment on various aspects of the paper that you may not see. Below, we provide two sample essays—one that is sloppy and another that is far better.

"Who we are depends far more on situational factors, such as our environment and our social context, than on our personality."

EXAMPLE 1: SLOPPY ESSAY

I believe that who we are depends on situational factors. After all, situations determine how we are to act in various situations. Not everyone can be expected to act according to their personality. Some environments have very strong norms about what the proper conduct should be. For example. In fraternity houses on U.S. campuses, there is a strong norm to drink a ton of alcohol. And students drink a lot of alcohol in such places. If who they are was determined only by their personality, then the nondrinkers should be not drinking, no matter the norms. But because of the strong norms to drink, even the nondrinkers feel that they have to drink and so they drink. Therefore, this proves that personality has nothing to do with who we are.

There are laws that force us to put aside our personality, and we are forced to act according to the law. For example. Some people may have a personality that makes them want to take lots of risks. So, they prefer to speed on the highway.

This is their personality. They are risk-takers. But they know that they can't speed because they will get caught. Because the law says that they are not allowed to speed. So, despite their personality, the environment determines whether they speed or not.

The topic for this essay is similar to the nature versus nurture debate. Some people believe that nature (our personality) determines who we are. Others believe that nurture (our environment) determines who we are. Because this is an ongoing debate, there is no clear answer about which side is correct.

There is some merit, however, to the fact that some of who we are is determined by our personality. After all, some people are known to be friendly, while others are known to be rude and unfriendly. This shows that personality is important.

So, the overall conclusion is that it depends on the context—sometimes people are governed by their personality while other times they are governed by their environment.

Now, let's analyze some of the problems in the paper.

The first two sentences are circular reasoning.

I believe that who we are depends on situational factors. After all, situations determine how we are to act in various situations. Not everyone can be expected to act according to their personality. Some environments have very strong norms about what the proper conduct should be. For example. In fraternity houses on U.S. campuses, there is a strong norm to drink a ton of alcohol. And students drink a lot of alcohol in such places. If who they are was determined only by their personality, then the nondrinkers should be not drinking, no matter the norms. But because of the strong norms to drink, even the nondrinkers feel that they have to drink and so they drink. Therefore, this proves that personality has nothing to do with who we are.

"For example" is a sentence fragment.

Good point but badly argued.

There are laws that force us to put aside our personality, and we are forced to act according to the law. For example. Some people may have a personality that makes them want to take lots of risks. So, they prefer to speed on the highway. This is their personality. They are risk-takers. But they know that they can't speed because they will get caught. Because the law says that they are not allowed to speed. So, despite their personality, the environment determines whether they speed or not.

"Proves" is too strong, as is "nothing."

Another good point, but a tighter case needs to be made for how lawful behavior relates to our personality.

The topic for this essay is similar to the nature versus nurture debate. Some people believe that nature (our personality) determines who we are. Others believe that nurture (our environment) determines who we are. Because this is an ongoing debate, there is no clear answer about which side is correct.

Nice example but wrong conclusion. It's possible to have an ongoing debate about something that has a clear answer.

There is some merit, however, to the fact that some of who we are is determined by our personality. After all, some people are known to be friendly, while others are known to be rude and unfriendly. This shows that personality is important.

This seems to contradict what was said earlier about the other side of the argument.

So, the overall conclusion is that it depends on the context—sometimes people are governed by their personality while other times they are governed by their environment.

This conclusion is unwarranted, given the strong position taken earlier.

EXAMPLE 2: SUPERIOR ESSAY

If we are to assume that the given statement is false—that in fact people's attitudes are determined by their internal characteristics—then we can expect people to hold the same attitude regardless of whom they are with, where they are, or in what context they are being asked to express their attitude. After all, if people's attitudes are determined by their internal characteristics, then the external context should not matter. People would then express the same attitude everywhere and in all contexts. This, however, is not the case.

Although I am not knowledgeable about findings from the social science research on this topic, I do know that I hold different attitudes on the same issue and that the nature of the attitude I hold depends very much on the context in which I express myself. For example, let us consider my attitude toward the rewards of hard work.

When I address my employees, I emphasize the fact that there is no other way to get ahead in life than through hard work. In order to motivate my employees, I tell them that there are no quick solutions and that good things come only to those who work hard, despite the challenges they face.

At other times, particularly when times are bad, it is difficult for me to believe that hard work always pays off. I have worked hard in my life, but I haven't been as successful as others who seem to have been in the right place at the right time.

My attitude toward hard work, thus, depends very much on external circumstances—whether I am in a good mood at the time, whether I am surrounded by successful or unsuccessful people, and so on. This shows that my attitude changes from situation to situation and hence is not determined by my internal characteristics.

Another problem with the premise that internal characteristics determine our attitude is that we do not know what is actually meant by "internal characteristics." Because these characteristics are "internal," we can never see them, and so we can never be quite sure that they actually exist. Hence, we can only infer that they exist, and this inference is based on measuring people's responses to questions designed to gauge their attitudes. In other words, we infer the existence of "internal characteristics" only when they impact attitudes; at other times, they are seen not to exist. This is circular reasoning—the logical end of the belief that internal characteristics determine our attitudes.

Day 15

Test 1, Part 3B: Argument Analysis Essay

Sample Topic

Assignment for Today:

Write an argument analysis on the given topic. Time limit: 30 minutes.

Discuss how well reasoned you find this argument.

The following appeared as an editorial article in Lincoln High School's newspaper.

"Our city government is neglecting the environment. We should elect Derek Gladstone as our Mayor because our current Mayor, Bob Livingworth, has done nothing to improve our environment. Derek Gladstone is a member of the Friends for a Friendly Planet. Unlike Bob Livingworth, Derek will protect our environment. Under Bob Livingworth's watch, we have seen a doubling of polluting industries in our city, our air has become much more polluted, and the local hospital has treated 25 percent more patients with respiratory illnesses. It is time to elect an environmentally friendly mayor and send a strong message to the city government."

Test 1, Part 3B: Argument Analysis Essay

Sample Essay Response

Assignment for Today:

Analyze your argument analysis from Day 15.

As mentioned previously, the best way to analyze your paper is to show it to someone else and ask for their feedback. Listed below are two passages, one that was written without much organization and another that is clearly superior.

"Our city government is neglecting the environment. We should elect Derek Gladstone as our Mayor because our current Mayor, Bob Livingworth, has done nothing to improve our environment. Derek Gladstone is a member of the Friends for a Friendly Planet. Unlike Bob Livingworth, Derek will protect our environment. Under Bob Livingworth's watch, we have seen a doubling of polluting industries in our city, our air has become much more polluted, and the local hospital has treated 25 percent more patients with respiratory illnesses. It is time to elect an environmentally friendly mayor and send a strong message to the city government."

EXAMPLE 1: SLOPPY ESSAY

All politicians are the same. All of them are after power, and we know that power corrupts. So, no matter who is elected mayor, that person is going to pursue his own self-interest anyway. There is little hope for the city to have cleaner air because industrial forces are far more powerful than the common citizen and industrial lobbyists will make sure that no real changes are made to introduce tougher environmental laws that would make the city cleaner.

So, we cannot trust what Bob Livingworth's opponents tell in their campaign promises. For that matter, we cannot trust most of the politicians and Bob Livingworth is also a politician. So, we cannot trust Livingworth and what he says in his campaign.

Friends for a Friendly Planet seems to be an organization that is dedicated to cleaning the air. If Livingworth becomes mayor, he may be able to clean the air because he would be obligated to the organization. But this is also unknown.

There is no question that the city has had many environmental problems—the air is dirtier, there are more polluting industries, and the local hospital is seeing an increase in respiratory problems. This means that the problems faced by the city are getting worse and worse. Some-thing clearly needs to be done, but I doubt that a new mayor will be very effective. After all, he is just a politician, and, as mentioned earlier, all politicians are corrupted by power.

The passage concludes that electing an environmentally friendly mayor will send a powerful message to the city government. This is probably true—after all, electing an environmentally friendly mayor is the first step in getting the city to enact tougher laws against air pollution. Only after we change the makeup of the city government can we hope for laws that reflect the will of the people.

The passage places a lot of emphasis on environmental issues. Environmental issues have to be balanced with economic issues, and the passage says nothing about the economic policies of either candidate. I'd like to know what economic policies each person endorses. After all, a radical environmental agenda is only one side of the equation. What about the economic agenda? People need jobs. And environmental policies cut the possibility of growth and therefore they stifle economic activity.

In summary, the passage is poorly written because it does not take into account the whole picture. It focuses exclusively on environmental issues and neglects other pressing issues that people are concerned about.

Now, let's analyze some of the problems in the paper.

Lots of hyperbole here. "All politicians" is too broad. Little justification for the claim that the new mayor will pursue "his own self-interest." "Industrial lobbyists" is never mentioned in the passage. This paragraph also has too many ideas.

All politicians are the same. All of them are after power, and we know that power corrupts. So, no matter who is elected mayor, that person is going to pursue his own self-interest anyway. There is little hope for the city to have cleaner air because industrial forces are far more powerful than the common citizen and industrial lobbyists will make sure that no real changes are made to introduce tougher environmental laws that would make the city cleaner.

Another unsubstantiated generalization—that we cannot trust politicians.

So, we cannot trust what Bob Livingworth's opponents tell in their campaign promises. For that matter, we cannot trust most of the politicians and Bob Livingworth is also a politician. So, we cannot trust Livingworth and what he says in his campaign.

No evidence in the passage about what the organization does. We know nothing about obligations from the passage.

Friends for a Friendly Planet seems to be an organization that is dedicated to cleaning the air. If Livingworth becomes mayor, he may be able to clean the air because he would be obligated to the organization. But this is also unknown.

Uncritical acceptance of the passage's claims—that pollution problems are getting worse.

There is no question that the city has had many environmental problems – the air is dirtier, there are more polluting industries, and the local hospital is seeing an increase in respiratory problems. This means that the problems faced by the city are getting worse and worse. Something clearly needs to be done, but I doubt that a new mayor will be very effective. After all, he is just a politician, and, as mentioned earlier, all politicians are corrupted by power.

Redundant—this was said earlier.

The passage concludes that electing an environmentally friendly mayor will send a powerful message to the city government. This is probably true – after all, electing an environmentally friendly mayor is the first step in getting the city to enact tougher laws against air pollution. Only after we change the makeup of the city government can we hope for laws that reflect the will of the people.

This is probably a suitable argument, though the point needs to be made more forcefully.

This paragraph has a good argument, but then it quickly degenerates into something irrelevant and unsubstantiated.

The passage places a lot of emphasis on environmental issues. Environmental issues have to be balanced with economic issues, and the passage says nothing about the economic policies of either candidate. I'd like to know

This analysis is based on only one point, and it neglects other arguments.

what economic policies each person endorses. After all, a radical environmental agenda is only one side of the equation. What about the economic agenda? People need jobs. And environmental policies cut the possibility of growth and therefore they stifle economic activity.

In summary, the passage is poorly written because it does not take into account the whole picture. It focuses exclusively on environmental issues and neglects other pressing issues that people are concerned about.

EXAMPLE 2: SUPERIOR ESSAY

In order to write a better essay, you should first get in the habit of organizing your thoughts and arguments. We urge you first to prepare a set of assumptions and/or conclusions that you will address in your essay. Then, each paragraph can be an elaboration of the central point. Here is an example of how this might be done.

Assumption 1: Friends for a Friendly Planet is an organization dedicated to working on environmental issues.

Assumption 2: Belonging to an organization means that members will follow the organization's mission.

Assumption 3: The environment can be controlled by the city government.

Assumption 4: Bob Livingworth had a direct hand in doubling the number of polluting industries, the deterioration of the air quality, and the rise in respiratory problems.

Assumption 5: The mayor has the power to reduce air pollution.

Assumption 6: The primary job of the mayor is to address environmental issues.

Conclusion: If elected, Derek Gladstone will be interested in and able to address environmental issues.

Based on the points noted above, here's what a sample essay might look like.

The given passage is based on a set of untenable or unsubstantiated assumptions. First, it assumes that Friends for a Friendly Planet is an environment-friendly organization. Many organizations adopt deceiving names, and one should be wary of equating the name of the organization with the implied mission of the organization. Based on the given passage, we have no way of knowing who constitutes this organization, what its mission is, or how it has acted in the past. For all we know, it may be a "front" put up by those seeking weaker environmental regulations.

Second, even if the Friends for a Friendly Planet were an organization genuinely interested in improving environmental conditions, we do not know whether members of the organization, once they acquire power, will keep their word. We have seen numerous politicians advocate term limits while running for office, only to abandon this position once they acquire power. Hence, there is little assurance in the passage that Derek Gladstone, if elected, will fulfill his obligation to enact environment-friendly legislation.

Third, we do not know anything about the environmental record of Bob Livingworth. Even though Livingworth is the current mayor, and even if we assume that the city government has endorsed environmentally unfriendly policies in the past, we do not know how Livingworth has voted on environmental issues. It may well be, for example, that he was the sole dissenting voice in the city government.

Fourth, the number of factories in the city may have doubled in the past year, but this alone does not establish the fact that they are the cause of increased air pollution. It could be that the adjacent town of Dirtyview has highly polluting industries, which means that, no matter what Mayor Livingworth's city does legislatively, its air quality is not going to improve unless the problems in Dirtyview are first addressed. On a similar note, the fact that local hospitals have treated 25 percent more patients with respiratory illnesses may indicate that hospitals in this city, because they are cheaper, are drawing more patients from Dirtyview.

Fifth, the passage assumes that environmental issues should be the sole concern of the mayor. Without further information about major issues facing the city, we do not know how much priority environmental issues should take.

Finally, even if Derek Gladstone is elected, it is unreasonable to assume that one person will solve the environmental problems in a city. We do not know, for example, what kinds of contracts the city has already signed with existing industries. It could be that the city has entered into agreements that would not allow any new changes to be made in how existing industries are operated or how much pollution they are allowed to emit. The bottom line here is that, because of all these unknown factors, it is impossible to tell whether the election of Derek Gladstone will make any difference in the city's pollution problems. Hence, the implied conclusion of the passage seems unwarranted.

Day 17

Test 1, Part 4: Math (2).

Questions and Answers

Assignment for Today:

Take the second part of a practice GRE Math Test under actual test conditions. Allow yourself exactly 30 minutes to complete the 30 questions in this test.

Directions: *For questions 1–15, each question contains two quantities—one on the left (Column A) and one on the right (Column B). Compare the quantities and answer*

(A) if Column A is greater than Column B

(B) if Column B is greater than Column A

(C) if the two columns are equal

(D) if you cannot determine a definite relationship from the information given

Never answer (E)

In some questions, information appears centered between the two columns. Centered information concerns each of the columns for that question only. Any symbol in one column represents the same value if it appears in the other column.

	Column A	Column B
1.	$\dfrac{3}{4} - \dfrac{2}{3}$	$\dfrac{3}{4} - \dfrac{2}{5}$
2.	$0.7p + 0.006q$	$0.7p + 0.06q$
3.	Area of a circle with radius π	Circumference of a circle with radius π

Column A	Column B

The number of cells in an organism doubles every hour. The organism has 1 cell at noon.

4.

Number of cells in the organism at 3:00 p.m. of the same day	6

The ratio $x{:}y$ is 3:5

5.

$15x$	$9y$

m, n, and p are factors of 60

$m \neq n \neq p$

6.

Highest possible value of the average (arithmetic mean) of m, n, and p	20

7.

$2ab - 1$	$4ab - 1$

Column A	Column B

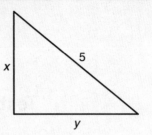

8.

$\sqrt{x^2+y^2}$	$\sqrt{5^2}$

m is a positive integer.

$$n = m\,(m + 1)\,(m + 2)$$

9.

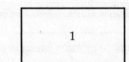

1	The remainder when n is divided by 6

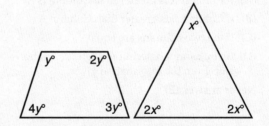

Note: Figure not drawn to scale

10.

y	x

Column A	Column B

11.

The number of integers between 8 and 8^4	The number of integers between -8 and $(-8)^4$

$n > 0$

12.

$\dfrac{n}{0.44}$	$\dfrac{0.56}{n}$

$x = -1$

13.

$\dfrac{5x + \frac{4}{3}}{3}$	$\dfrac{4x + \frac{5}{3}}{3}$

Let #x# denote the sum of the tens digit of x and the units digit of x. For example, #14# = 1 + 4 = 5.

Let {y} denote #y + 5#. For example, {19} = #24# = 2 + 4 = 6.

14.

{53} − #44#	53 − 44

Column A	Column B

The six sides of a cube are each assigned a different number between 1 and 6, and the cube is tossed without any systematic pattern.

15.

The probability that the cube will land on the same side twice in a row	The probability that the cube will land on the number 3 twice in a row

Directions: *For questions 16–30, solve each problem, and select the appropriate answer choice, A–E. Circle the letter of your choice.*

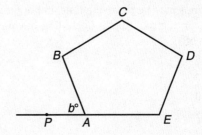

16. *ABCDE* is a regular pentagon. What is the measure of angle *PAB*, denoted by *b*, in the figure above?

   (A) 36

   (B) 72

   (C) 100

   (D) 108

   (E) It cannot be determined.

17. A square with a diagonal of length $5\sqrt{2}$ has the same area as circle O. What is the radius of circle O?

    (A) $\dfrac{5}{\sqrt{\pi}}$

    (B) $\dfrac{5}{2\sqrt{\pi}}$

    (C) $\dfrac{25}{2\pi}$

    (D) $\dfrac{25}{\pi}$

    (E) 5

18. Five lamps, each with a different colored light bulb, are used to light up a room. If each lamp can be either on or off, and any combination of the lamps may be on at one time, in how many ways can the room be lit (including having all lamps off)?

    (A) 5

    (B) 7

    (C) 10

    (D) 25

    (E) 32

19. Jerry, Kerry, and Larry divide 60 jelly beans among themselves in the ratio 3:4:5, respectively. The number of jelly beans Larry got was how many more than the average number (arithmetic mean) of jelly beans that each person got?

    (A) 1

    (B) 5

    (C) 7

    (D) 13

    (E) 25

20. If x and y are factors of 24, what is the least possible value of their sum?

    (A) −25

    (B) −24

    (C) 10

    (D) 11

    (E) 24

Questions 21–26 are based on the following figure.

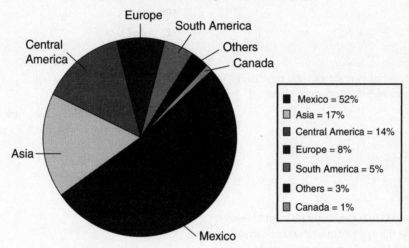

New Immigrants in California by
Country of Origin, 1985
(Total number of immigrants = 1.5 million)

Mexico = 52%
Asia = 17%
Central America = 14%
Europe = 8%
South America = 5%
Others = 3%
Canada = 1%

Central America	
El Salvador	97,000
Nicaragua	83,000
Honduras	18,000
Guatemala	8,000
Others	4,000

South America	
Colombia	34,000
Ecuador	24,000
Peru	10,000
Others	7,000

Asia	
Philippines	109,000
India	42,000
Israel	38,000
Iran	33,000
China	21,000
Others	12,000

Europe	
Italy	42,000
France	33,000
Portugal	19,000
Ireland	14,000
Others	12,000

21. According to the chart, approximately how many new immigrants were from Mexico in 1985?

   (A) 52,000
   (B) 78,000
   (C) 520,000
   (D) 720,000
   (E) 780,000

22. New immigrants from the Philippines represent approximately what percent of new Asian immigrants?

   (A) 7
   (B) 17
   (C) 43
   (D) 87
   (E) 109

23. Approximately how many more new immigrants are from Europe than from South America?

    (A) 45,000
    (B) 75,000
    (C) 195,000
    (D) 300,000
    (E) 450,000

24. Approximately what percent of total new immigrants were from El Salvador and Colombia?

    (A) 9
    (B) 13
    (C) 19
    (D) 28
    (E) 46

25. If there were 480,000 new immigrants from Mexico in 1984, what is the approximate percent increase in the number of new immigrants from Mexico from 1984 to 1985?

    (A) 38
    (B) 62
    (C) 109
    (D) 162
    (E) 217

26. If $a(8 - 5) = 8 - \dfrac{5}{a}$, then what is a possible value for a?

    (A) $-\dfrac{5}{3}$
    (B) -1
    (C) $\dfrac{5}{3}$
    (D) 5
    (E) 8

27. If $5{,}050 \times 0.5y = 126{,}250$, then $5{,}050 \div y^2 =$

    (A) 2.02
    (B) 2.2
    (C) 101
    (D) 202
    (E) 12,625,000

$$P = 4{,}900 \times 10^n$$
$$-3 < n < 3$$

28. According to the rules above, how many different integer values of n will make P a perfect square?

    (A) 1
    (B) 2
    (C) 3
    (D) 4
    (E) 5

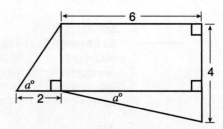

29. The figure above consists of two right triangles and one rectangle. What is the area of the figure?

    (A) 12
    (B) 16
    (C) 20
    (D) 24
    (E) It cannot be determined.

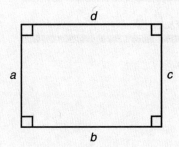

Note: Figure not drawn to scale.

30. What is one half the perimeter of the rectangle with
sides a, b, c, and d if its area is 50 and $a^2 + b^2 = 125$?

   (A) 15
   (B) $15\sqrt{2}$
   (C) 25
   (D) 30
   (E) 225

Quick Answer Guide

Test 1, Part 4: Math (2)

1. B	9. A	17. A	25. B
2. D	10. C	18. E	26. C
3. A	11. B	19. B	27. A
4. A	12. D	20. A	28. C
5. C	13. B	21. E	29. B
6. A	14. B	22. C	30. A
7. D	15. A	23. A	
8. D	16. B	24. A	

For explanations to these questions, see Day 18.

Day 18

Test 1, Part 4: Math (2).
Explanations and Strategies

Assignment for Today:

Review the explanations for the Math Test you took on Day 17.

---

1. The correct answer is (B).

Notice that "$\frac{3}{4}$" is in both columns. So, we can eliminate this term and not even consider it. So, we're really comparing $-\frac{2}{3}$ in Column A and $-\frac{2}{5}$ in Column B.

We know that $\frac{2}{3}$ is approximately .667. So, $-\frac{2}{3}$ is about -0.667. And, $\frac{2}{5}$ is 0.4. So, $-\frac{2}{5}$ is -0.4.

So, Column A = -0.667. Column B = -0.4. Then, Column B is greater because it's a smaller negative number.

2. The correct answer is (D).

Both columns have the quantity $0.7p$, and so we can get rid of it from both sides. Then we are really comparing $0.006q$ in Column A and $0.06q$ in Column B.

Let's plug in values for q and compare the columns.

If $q = 0$, in Column A, $0.006q = 0$ and in Column B, $0.06q = 0$.

This says that both columns are equal.

But, if $q = 1$, then $0.006q = 0.006$ (Column A) and $0.06q = 0.06$ (Column B), and so Column B is greater. Because we get two different results, we can conclude that the correct answer is (D).

3. The correct answer is (A).

For Column A, we need to find the area of a circle with radius π. We know that the area of a circle is πr^2, where r is the radius. If we take the radius of the circle to be π,

Column A = Area of circle = $\pi r^2 = \pi(\pi)^2 = \pi^3$.

Circumference of a circle is given by the formula: $2\pi r$. If π is the radius, then,

Column B = Circumference of circle = $2\pi r = 2\pi(\pi) = 2\pi^2$.

So, we're comparing π^3 in Column A with $2\pi^2$ in Column B. Notice that we can divide out π^2 from both sides, so that we compare π in Column A with 2 in Column B.

Then Column A = $\pi = 3.14$ and Column B = 2. So, Column A is greater.

4. The correct answer is (A).

If the organism has 1 cell at noon, then, at 1:00 p.m., it will have 2 cells (double of 1). At 2:00 p.m., it will have 4 cells (double of 2), and at 3:00 p.m., it will have 8 cells (double of 4). So, Column A is greater than Column B.

5.   The correct answer is (C).

To solve this problem, we can first find an equation that relates x and y. Because x:y is 3:5, we can say

$$\frac{x}{y} = \frac{3}{5}$$

$$5x = 3y$$

Solving for x, we get

$$x = \frac{3}{5}y$$

To determine the value of $15x$ in terms of y, we can multiply both sides of this equation by 15, giving us:

$$15x = \frac{15 \times 3}{5}y$$

$$= 9y$$

Here we see that $15x$ equals $9y$, so the values in both columns are equal.

6.   The correct answer is (A).

Let's first find the factors of 60. The easiest way is to start from 1 and list all numbers that divide evenly into 60. They are 1, 2, 3, 4, 5, 6, 10, 12, 15, 20, 30, and 60.

On the test, to see if you have all the factors or not, take the first number (1) and multiply it by the last (60), take the second number (2) and multiply it by the second from the last (30), and work your way inward. All the products should be 60. For example, 1×60, 2×30, 3×20, 4×15, 5×12, and 6×10 all give you 60.

Anyway, to find the largest possible value of the average, take the three largest factors—20, 30, and 60. Their sum is $20 + 30 + 60 = 110$. Their average is $110 \div 3 = 36$ and change.

So, Column A is slightly more than 36 and Column B is 20. So, Column A is greater than Column B.

7.   The correct answer is (D).

Let's first eliminate the "–1" from each side. (You can always eliminate equal numbers, but not necessarily equal letters, from each side.) So, we're really comparing $2ab$ in Column A with $4ab$ in Column B.

Now let's plug in our special value of zero for either a or b. If $a = 0$, Column A = 0 and Column B = 0. So, the columns could be equal. Now let's plug in 1 for a and b. Then, Column A = $2(1)(1) = 2$, and column B = $4(1)(1) = 4$. Now B is greater than A.

As soon as we get two different results, the answer has to be choice (D), cannot be determined.

8.   The correct answer is (D).

This triangle looks like it's a right triangle. BUT, there's nothing that says it is. So watch it!

IF the triangle were a right triangle AND if 5 were the hypotenuse, then Columns A and B would be equal. But, in the given triangle, we have no way of knowing.

For example, if $x = 2$ and $y = 4$, then Column A would be equal to $\sqrt{20}$ and Column B would be equal to $\sqrt{25}$, which means Column B would be greater. But what would happen if $x = 3$ and $y = 5$? Then, Column A would be greater. This tells us that the correct answer is (D).

9.   The correct answer is (A).

The best way to do this problem is to plug in values for m. Let's say that m is 1. Then, $n = 1 \times 2 \times 3 = 6$. The remainder when 6 is divided by 6 is 0, and so Column B is 0. Then, Column A is greater than Column B.

If m is 2, then $n = 2 \times 3 \times 4 = 24$. Again, the remainder (when 24 is divided by 6) is zero, and so Column A is greater than Column B.

If m is 3, then $n = 3 \times 4 \times 5 = 60$. The remainder is again 0, and Column A is greater than Column B.

We could try this a couple of more times, but we'll find that n will always be a multiple of 6. In other words, n divided by 6 will always have a remainder of 0. So, Column A will always be greater than Column B.

10. The correct answer is (C).

To solve this problem, we must know that the sum of all the interior angles of any figure is $180(n - 2)$, where n is the number of sides. In a triangle, $n = 3$, and so the sum of all angles is $180(3 - 2)$, which is $180(1)$, or $180°$.

Let's apply this to Column B. We know that all three angles have to add up to 180°. That is, $x + 2x + 2x = 180$

Or, $5x = 180$

Then, $x = 36°$.

So,   Column B is 36°

Let's use our formula to find the sum of all interior angles in Column A. The figure has four sides, and so $n = 4$. Then, the sum of all interior angles is $180(4 - 2) = 180(2) = 360°$.

There are four different angles. Let's add them up and make the sum equal to 360°.

Then $y + 2y + 3y + 4y = 360$

That is, $10y = 360$

Or, $y = 36°$

So,   Column A = Column B = 36°

The correct answer is choice (C).

11. The correct answer is (B).

Let's work this problem in terms of a number line. Then, the integers described in Column A go from positive 8 to 8^4. All of them lie on the positive side of the number line.

To work Column B, we need to remember that a negative number taken to an *even* power is *positive*. For example, $(-3)^2$ is positive 9. So, $(-8)^4$ is a positive number, and in fact $(-8)^4 = 8^4$. So, in terms of our number line, the integers described in Column B go from -8 to 8^4. Clearly, there are more integers in Column B because Column B includes the negative integers from -8 to 0, whereas Column A doesn't.

12. The correct answer is (D).

We know that n is a positive number. So, let's plug in different positive values for n and see what answers we get.

To make things easy, let's first plug $n = 0.44$. That way, we can divide the numerator and denominator in Column A to get 1.

If $n = 0.44$, Column A $= \dfrac{0.44}{0.44} = 1$.

Column B $= \dfrac{0.56}{0.44}$, which is greater than 1 (because it's a top-heavy fraction).

So, when $n = 0.44$, Column B is greater than Column A.

Now let's try $n = 0.56$ (so that we can divide the numerator and the denominator in Column B to get 1).

If $n = 0.56$, Column A $= \dfrac{0.56}{0.44} > 1$ (top-heavy fraction).

Column B $= \dfrac{0.56}{0.56} = 1$.

Now Column A is greater than Column B. Because we get two different results, the right answer is choice (D).

13. The correct answer is (B).

Before we plug in values for x, we can eliminate the 3s in the denominator from both sides. So, we are really comparing:

$5x + \dfrac{4}{3}$ in Column A and $4x + \dfrac{5}{3}$ in Column B.

Now, let's plug in the value of $x = -1$.

Column A $= -5 + \dfrac{4}{3} \approx -5 + 1.33 = -3.67$

Column B $= -4 + \dfrac{5}{3} \approx -4 + 1.67 = -2.33$

Because Column B has a smaller negative number, Column B is greater.

14. The correct answer is (B).

Column B is easy. It's $53 - 44 = 9$.

Now, let's work Column A.

{53} = #53 + 5# = #58# = 5 + 8 = 13. And #44# = 4 + 4 = 8. So,

{53} – #44# = 13 – 8 = 5. Therefore, Column A is 5 and Column B is 9, and Column B is greater than Column A.

15. The correct answer is (A).

An easy way to solve probability problems is to use the formula:

$$\text{probability} = \frac{\text{favored outcome}}{\text{total outcomes}}$$

The trick here is to find the total number of outcomes. If we toss a cube once, there are six possible ways the cube could land: 1–2–3–4–5–6. For every number that comes up on the first toss, there are six possibilities for the second toss. That is, if 1 comes up the first time, there are six possibilities for the second: 1–2–3–4–5–6. This is true for every side of the cube, as shown in the diagram below:

Toss #1	Possibilities for Toss #2
1	1 2 3 4 5 6
2	1 2 3 4 5 6
3	1 2 3 4 5 6
4	1 2 3 4 5 6
5	1 2 3 4 5 6
6	1 2 3 4 5 6

There are a total of 36 ways the cube can land.
In Column A, there are six favored outcomes (1-1, 2-2, 3-3, etc.) and so the probability is: $\frac{6}{36}$, or $\frac{1}{6}$.
In Column B, there is only one favored outcome (3-3), and so the probability is $\frac{1}{36}$. So, Column A is greater.

16. The correct answer is (B). 72

We're told this is a *regular* pentagon, which means all sides are equal and so all interior angles are equal. To find the total interior angle of a figure, we can use the formula:

Interior angle = $180(n-2)$, where n is the number of sides in the figure.

If you forget the formula, think about a triangle, for which $n = 3$ because it has 3 sides. Then the formula gives you $180(3-2)$, which is $180(1)$, or 180.

In a pentagon, $n = 5$ because it has five sides. Then,

Interior angle = $180(5-2) = 180(3) = 540$

This is the sum of all interior angles. Because there are five such angles, each interior angle is 540 ÷ 5, which is 108°.

But 108° is not the right answer, mind you. We're asked for angle b. Notice that PAE forms a straight line. If angle EAB is 108° (1 interior angle), then angle b must be $180 - 108 = 72°$, which is choice (B).

An alternative way to do this problem is to remember the exterior angles of any regular polygon add up to 360°. Since, in this case, there are 5 exterior angles, 360 ÷ 50 = 72°, which is choice (B).

17. The correct answer is (A). $\dfrac{5}{\sqrt{\pi}}$

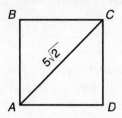

For problems like this, it's helpful to draw a diagram, such as the one shown above. We're told that diagonal $\overline{AC}$ of square $ABCD$ has measure $5\sqrt{2}$. Notice that side AD is equal to side CD (both are sides of a square) and, in the triangle ADC, $\overline{AC}$ is the hypotenuse. Let's say $CD = x = AD$.

Then, $(5\sqrt{2})^2 = x^2 + x^2 = 2x^2$

Taking the square root, we get $5\sqrt{2} = \sqrt{2}\,x$.

We can divide the $\sqrt{2}$ from both sides of the equation so that

$5 = x$

Actually, we could have found the length of $\overline{CD}$ by noting that $\triangle ADC$ is a 45-45-90 triangle whose hypotenuse is $\sqrt{2}$ times the length of one of the sides.

So, the length of each side of the square is 5. Then, its area is 25. We're told that the circle has the same area as the square. So, if the area of the square is 25, the area of the circle is also 25. Now, let's plug 25 into the formula for the area of a circle, πr^2, so that:

$25 = \pi r^2$

Dividing by π, we get $\dfrac{25}{\pi} = r^2$.

Taking the square root, $\dfrac{5}{\sqrt{\pi}} = r$, which is the answer.

18. The correct answer is (E). 32

We see that any lamp may be either on or off, so in deciding how to light the room, for each lamp we must choose one of two possible choices. To count the number of ways that more than one lamp can light the room, we *multiply* the number of choices together.

For example, with two lamps, there are *four* possibilities: both lamps off, both lamps on, the first lamp on and the second lamp off, and the first lamp off with the second lamp on. With three lamps, there are eight combinations. With four lamps, there are 16 combinations. And with five lamps, there are 32 possible ways of having the lamps on and off.

As each lamp has two possible modes (on or off), the math is:

$2 \times 2 \times 2 \times 2 \times 2 = 2^5 = 32$

19. The correct answer is (B). 5

Let's first figure out the sum of the three individual ratio numbers, which is $3 + 4 + 5 = 12$. Then,

Jerry got $\dfrac{3}{12} \times 60 = 15$ jelly beans,

Kerry got $\dfrac{4}{12} \times 60 = 20$ jelly beans,

and Larry got $\dfrac{5}{12} \times 60 = 25$ jelly beans.

Check to see that these three numbers add up to 60 ($15 + 20 + 25 = 60$).

We know that there was a total of 60 jelly beans shared by three people. Then, the average number of jelly beans each person got has to be $60 \div 3 = 20$. So, Larry got $25 - 20 = 5$ more than the average, which is choice (B).

20. The correct answer is (A). –25

Let's look at the choices: two negative numbers. This should give us a clue. Remember, -24×-1 gives us 24. So, both –24 and –1 are factors of 24. Now the problem is easy. The lowest value of the sum of two factors of 24 is $(-24 + -1)$, which is equal to –25, choice (A).

21. The correct answer is (E). 780,000

The title of the chart says that the total number of new immigrants was 1.5 million. We know from the chart that 52% of new immigrants were from Mexico. So, the number of new immigrants from Mexico = 52% of 1.5 million = 52% of 1,500,000.

Notice that 52% means slightly greater than half of 1.5 million. We know that half of 1.5 million is 750,000. Now we should look for an answer that is slightly greater than 750,000. So, the closest answer would be choice (E), 780,000.

22. The correct answer is (C). 43

Let's first find the total number of immigrants from Asia.

Total Asian immigrants = $109,000 + 42,000 + 38,000 + 33,000 + 21,000 + 12,000$

$= 255,000$

We know that the total number of immigrants from the Philippines is 109,000. So, now we need to answer the question: 109,000 is what percent of 255,000?

Notice that half (or 50%) of 255,000 would have been about 125,000. So, we can approximate 109,000 as a little below 50%. Now look for an answer that is slightly below 50%. Choice (C), 43, is the best answer.

23. The correct answer is (A). 45,000

Of all new immigrants, 8% were from Europe and 5% were from South America. So, there were 8% – 5% = 3% more immigrants from Europe than South America. We know that the total number of new immigrants is 1.5 million. So, now we should find 3% of 1.5 million.

Then, 3% of 1.5 million = $.03 \times 1,500,000$

$= 45,000$.

24. The correct answer is (A). 9

From the figure, we see that 97,000 new immigrants came from El Salvador and 34,000 new immigrants came from Colombia. Thus, a total of 131,000 new immigrants came from El Salvador and Colombia combined. We know that there were a total of 1.5 million new immigrants. So, now the question is:

131,000 is what percent of 1.5 million? To find the required percent, we can use the formula:

$$\text{Required percent} = \frac{131,000}{1,500,000} \times 100$$

$$= \frac{131}{1,500} \times 100 = \frac{131}{15} \approx 9$$

So, the correct answer is choice (A), 9.

25. The correct answer is (B). 62

In 1985, from the figure, 52% of all new immigrants were from Mexico. We know that the total number of new immigrants was 1.5 million. So, the total number of new immigrants from Mexico in 1985 = 52% of 1.5 million = .52 × 1.5 million = .78 million = 780,000.

In 1984, the number of new immigrants from Mexico was 480,000. Then, the increase in the number of new immigrants from Mexico = 780,000 − 480,000 = 300,000. To find the percent increase, we can use the formula:

$$\text{percent increase} = \frac{\text{increase}}{\text{number in 1984}} \times 100$$

$$= \frac{300,000}{480,000} \times 100 = \frac{300}{480} \times 100 = \frac{30}{48} \times 100$$

$$= \frac{5}{8} \times 100$$

$$= 62.5\%$$

So, the closest answer is choice (B), 62.

26. The correct answer is (C). $\frac{5}{3}$

The easiest way to work this problem is to plug the value for a back into the problem and see if it works. Before we do that, let's simplify the given equation. So that

$$a(8-5) = 8 - \frac{5}{a} \text{ becomes}$$

$$3a = 8 - \frac{5}{a}$$

As usual, we start from choice (C). So, let's plug

in $a = \frac{5}{3}$. Then, $3 \times \frac{5}{3} = 8 - \dfrac{5}{\frac{5}{3}}$

Or, $5 = 8 - 5 \times \dfrac{3}{5}$

Or, $5 = 8 - 3 = 5$

So, this value of a works and choice (C) is the right answer.

27. The correct answer is (A). 2.02

We are given:

$$5,050 \times 0.5y = 126,250$$

Dividing both sides by 5,050, we get:

$$0.5y = 25$$

Dividing both sides by 0.5, we get:

$$y = 50$$

Now that we know the value of y, we can solve the problem:

$$5,050 \div y^2 = 5,050 \div (50)^2 = 5,050 \div 2,500$$

$$= \frac{5,050}{2,500}$$

$$= 2.02$$

28. The correct answer is (C). 3

Not an easy problem, that's for sure. The key is to realize that 49 will be a perfect square if it has 0, 2, 4, 6, 8, . . . zeros after it. In other words, 49 (no zeros) is a perfect square (7 × 7), 4,900 (two zeros) is a perfect square (70 × 70), 490,000 (four zeros) is a perfect square (700 × 700), and so on.

So, let's plug in values for n, remembering that n can be equal to −2, −1, 0, 1, or 2. Don't forget: n cannot equal −3 or 3.

If $n = -2$, $P = 4,900 \times 10^n = 4,900 \times 10^{-2} = 49$. (A perfect square)

(When you multiply by 10^{-2}, it's like dividing by 100.)

If $n = -1$, $P = 4,900 \times 10^{-1} = 490$. (Not a perfect square)

If $n = 0$, $P = 4,900 \times 10^0 = 4,900$. (A perfect square)

(Multiplying by 10^0 is the same as multiplying by 1 because anything raised to the power of 0 is equal to 1.)

If $n = 1$, $P = 4,900 \times 10^1 = 49,000$. (Not a perfect square)

If $n = 2$, $P = 4,900 \times 10^2 = 490,000$. (A perfect square)

There are three perfect squares (when $n = -2, 0$, or 2), which means n can have three different values.

29. The correct answer is (B). 16

The trick to this problem is to rearrange the two triangles and one rectangle to form one large right triangle. Two possible results are:

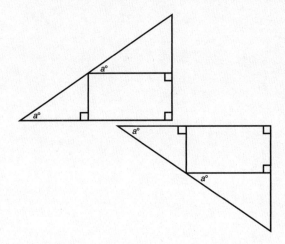

We know this is a right triangle because the two angles labeled a are equal and both start from parallel lines (the rectangle's sides).

With the newly drawn figure, we use $A = \frac{1}{2}bh$ to calculate the area of the large right triangle:

$$A = \frac{1}{2}bh$$
$$= \frac{1}{2} \times (6+2) \times 4$$
$$= 16$$

30. The correct answer is (A). 15

The perimeter of the rectangle is $a + b + c + d$, which is the same as $2(a + b)$. In other words, $(a + b)$ is half the perimeter.

Note also that $(a + b)^2 = a^2 + b^2 + 2ab$. But $(a + b)$ is half the perimeter. So, we can write the above equation as:

(half the perimeter)$^2 = a^2 + b^2 + 2ab$. Call this equation #1.

But we are told that $a^2 + b^2 = 125$. Also, the area of the rectangle is ab, which we are told is 50. Then $2ab = 100$.

Let's substitute these two values in equation #1. We get:

(half the perimeter)$^2 = 125 + 100 = 225$. That is,

(half the perimeter) $= \sqrt{225}$, which is 15, choice (A).

Test 1, Part 5: Verbal (2).

Questions and Answers

Assignment for Today:

Take the second part of a practice GRE Verbal Test under actual test conditions. Allow yourself exactly 30 minutes to complete the 38 questions in the test.

Directions: For questions 1–7, one or more words have been left out of each sentence. Circle the answer, A–E, that contains the word or words that best fit the meaning of the entire sentence.

1. The president's speech contained common words and simple examples mainly because her advisers counseled her to be more _____ instead of being so erudite.

    (A) accessible
    (B) gregarious
    (C) mercenary
    (D) sanctimonious
    (E) saturnine

2. Soon after Mary ascended the English throne in 1553, Parliament voted to reinstate the medieval law that _____ heresy by burning the perpetrator at the stake.

    (A) rewarded
    (B) mollified
    (C) usurped
    (D) punished
    (E) welcomed

3. During the final meeting of the convention, the chairperson _____ that nominations to _____ a party candidate would begin.

    (A) observed..hire
    (B) lamented..constrain
    (C) indicated..impoverish
    (D) clarified..congratulate
    (E) announced..elect

4. The Olympic gold medalist found that her fame was _____ because by the time she arrived home, no one even remembered what she had achieved.

    (A) resilient
    (B) salient
    (C) ephemeral
    (D) lascivious
    (E) lucrative

5. The Sophists taught that influencing forces can be ____ systematically and can be understood through the use of a ____ mind.

   (A) mitigated..banal

   (B) analyzed..disciplined

   (C) conjectured..controlled

   (D) dispelled..decrepit

   (E) categorized..charlatan

6. The owner of the small-town movie theater was a(n) ____ man who regularly ____ films he thought would be objectionable to his conservative clientele.

   (A) pious..expurgated

   (B) avaricious..promoted

   (C) fastidious..emasculated

   (D) disputatious..censored

   (E) churlish..attenuated

7. The clearest symbol of the village architect is not a ____ for a simple facade, but the automatic allocation of space for an outhouse that stems from a long and deeply ____ way of life.

   (A) penchant..ingrained

   (B) prescription..unsanitary

   (C) decree..treasured

   (D) propensity..urban

   (E) yearning..nascent

Directions: *For questions 8–16, determine the relationship between the two words given in capital letters. Then, from the choices listed A–E, select the one pair that has a relationship most similar to that of the capitalized pair. Circle the letter of that pair.*

---

8. TRUCK:HAUL::

   (A) bicycle:race

   (B) towel:clean

   (C) mentor:guide

   (D) road:detour

   (E) synapse:feel

9. FAMINE:FOOD::

   (A) feast:fowl

   (B) market:stall

   (C) drought:rain

   (D) shoe:foot

   (E) cough:wheeze

10. VINTNER:WINE::

    (A) professor:students

    (B) poet:anthologies

    (C) historian:artifacts

    (D) physicist:trees

    (E) baker:bread

11. SPACE:COSMONAUT::

    (A) kitchen:utensil

    (B) hangar:pilot

    (C) building:architect

    (D) frontier:pioneer

    (E) market:grocer

12. OFFICE:METIER::

    (A) sauna:sweat

    (B) leisure:home

    (C) engine:power

    (D) atelier:artistry

    (E) moat:water

13. TOURNIQUET:BLOOD::

    (A) thermometer:fever

    (B) computer:information

    (C) ligature:stitch

    (D) moratorium:repayment

    (E) check:money

14. PROMISCUOUS:HARLOT::

    (A) puissant:stallion

    (B) materialistic:bourgeois

    (C) pernicious:detective

    (D) incorrigible:thief

    (E) sleazy:hotel

15. PLENARY:ASSEMBLY::

 (A) bountiful:harvest

 (B) saturated:solution

 (C) legislative:council

 (D) terrestrial:earth

 (E) constitutional:monarchy

16. CIRCUMSPECT:INDECOROUS::

 (A) circumambient:surrounded

 (B) circumstantial:incidental

 (C) circumnavigable:global

 (D) circumlocutory:terse

 (E) circumvolutory:coiled

Directions: Read each passage and answer the questions that follow. Base your answers only on what is stated or implied in the passage.

Questions 17–20 are based on the following passage.

If we only had a Walt Whitman for London! Whitman is one of the voices of the earth, and it is only in Whitman that the paving stones really speak, with a voice as authentic as the voice of
(5) the hills. He knew no distinction between what is called the work of nature and what is the work of man. He left out nothing; what still puzzles us is the blind, loving, embracing way in which he brings crude names and things into his vision—
(10) the name of a trade, a street, a territory—no matter what syllables it might carry along with it. He created a vital poetry of cities. It was only a part of what he did; but since Whitman there is no gainsaying it any more.
(15)   It has been said of Whitman that he is mere bathybius, that he is in literature in the condition of protoplasm, that he is a maker of poems in solution, and that he remains an expanse of crystallizable substances, waiting for the structural
(20) change that never came. I think that Stendhal invented the latter phrase in his cold and penetrating study of the physiology of love, *De l' Amour.* He discovered for himself a method of

unemotional, minute, slightly ironical analysis,
(25) which has fascinated modern minds.
    In the case of Whitman, what is evident in his pages is that men played a greater part in his life's drama than women. As his life is a mixture of lawful and lawless propensities and rebellious
(30) instincts, there is no coordination in his vagabond existence between such clashing qualities in so strange a temperament. He gives one an extraordinary sense of bodily sensations. He sees nothing really spiritual in flesh—he is too much
(35) of a materialist. Certain of his vices are indecent; yet how often one sees in nature indecency! To be immodest or prurient is an inherent vice: Whitman is neither.

17. The author apparently believes that Walt Whitman's writing is

 (A) cold and penetrating.

 (B) immodest and prurient.

 (C) quixotic and whimsical.

 (D) earthy and authentic.

 (E) obscure and forgotten.

18. Which of the following best describes the author's tone in the discussion of Whitman's writing?

 (A) Sarcastic

 (B) Laudatory

 (C) Disparaging

 (D) Droll

 (E) Dispassionate

19. Which of the following statements about Whitman can be inferred from the passage?

 (A) He lived a life of hermetic solitude.

 (B) He spent much of his time in cafés.

 (C) He wrote honestly, if indecently.

 (D) He wrote extensively about his romances with women.

 (E) He saw the world chiefly in spiritual terms.

20. The phrase "mere bathybius" in lines 15–16 is used in the passage to indicate the

    (A) clarity of Whitman's prose and poetry.

    (B) unsurpassed literary genius of Whitman.

    (C) uncategorizable nature of Whitman's talent.

    (D) prototypicality of Whitman's genius.

    (E) fascinating nonsentimentality of Whitman's mind.

Questions 21–27 are based on the following passage.

The undergraduate college, during the last two decades, has been the target of a great deal of miscellaneous criticism, and no one knows as well as those on the inside how much it is de-
(5) served. The college has been accused, in some cases with reason, of crimes against almost all nature of educational misdemeanors and felonies: of laxness in teaching, of flabbiness in discipline, of prehistoric business methods; of
(10) overemphasis on athletics; of providing opportunities for falsified and dubious research; and, in general, of a failure to comprehend and to meet its responsibilities. That many of the attacks upon it have been unintelligent there can be no
(15) doubt, but the discussion aroused, even by such biased caviling, has been helpful and stimulating.

It is a curious but undoubted fact that the stimulus leading to the reformation of institutions very seldom comes from within. Whether
(20) it be the church, the business corporation, the governmental office, or the school, some outside irritation seems to be necessary before the inertia of custom can be shaken off. So, too, it is with the university; only recently have the criticisms
(25) and barbs of non-academicians moved the academy to reconsider its goals and operations.

The progress made during the last several decades has certainly been enormous, and it is still going on. In the better institutions, there has been
(30) little less than a revolution. As to the others, the process of improvement is very rapid.

Mr. Keppel's review of the results achieved—and of the present state of undergraduate instruction throughout the country—is very timely as
(35) well as exceedingly interesting. His experience as secretary of Columbia University and dean of Columbia College has given him contact with all phases of educational administration. He approaches his subject with a clear mind, with free-
(40) dom from insularity and complete acquaintance with educational progress, so that his book is an authoritative statement of the present stage of the evolution of our undergraduate institutions. He has, withal, an understanding of the psychology
(45) of college students, a thorough and sympathetic appreciation of their virtues, their foibles, and their needs, and he never fails to keep in mind the fact that the college must be adapted to the student, rather than the student to the college.

(50) The book opens with an analysis of the various types of institutions offering the bachelor's degree, and of the strengths and weaknesses of each of these types. This is followed by a discussion of the raw material with which the college
(55) works: the equipment—moral, intellectual and physical—which students bring with them, the social organization of student life, their athletics, and their religious, moral, and intellectual development. Mr. Keppel then passes to a
(60) consideration of the administrative and educational machinery of the college and to its finished product, the alumni.

There can be no doubt that the tone of student life has greatly improved during the last 20 years.
(65) There is much less alcohol abuse than there once was, less boisterousness and less lawlessness. If morality has declined, there is a larger emphasis on the social obligation of the individual. Although some of us, but not Mr. Keppel, believe
(70) that intercollegiate athletics, as presently conducted, cost more than they are worth, we are very ready to admit that even here there has been improvement.

21. The primary purpose of this passage is to

    (A) delineate the virtues of the best colleges.

    (B) critique undergraduate education.

    (C) review a recently published book.

    (D) show how education has changed in the past two decades.

    (E) demonstrate the eroding social fabric of the United States.

22. According to the passage, undergraduate education has recently been accused of all of the following EXCEPT

    (A) lazy teaching.

    (B) fabricated research.

    (C) outdated business methods.

    (D) disregard for student needs.

    (E) neglected responsibilities.

23. The word "dubious" in line 11 is used to mean

    (A) dishonest.

    (B) ambiguous.

    (C) doubtful.

    (D) vague.

    (E) questionable.

24. The author implies that a university is similar to a church in that both

    (A) require outside impetus to bring about internal change.

    (B) are leaders in advocating social causes.

    (C) discipline their members to achieve a higher aim.

    (D) must be adapted to fit the needs of their members.

    (E) put top priority on teaching social responsibility.

25. In comparing the progress made in universities during the last several decades, the passage implies that

    (A) better institutions have a long way to go before they can lay claim to a revolution.

    (B) better institutions have changed more.

    (C) private colleges have resisted the trend to change.

    (D) Mr. Keppel has outlined ten key steps to success.

    (E) non-academicians have overstepped their boundaries.

26. In describing the qualifications of Mr. Keppel, the passage mentions all of the following EXCEPT that he

    (A) was dean of Columbia College.

    (B) understands how students think.

    (C) has studied evolution in present stages.

    (D) is sympathetic to college students.

    (E) is a good thinker.

27. According to the passage, Mr. Keppel believes that intercollegiate athletic programs

    (A) cost more than they are worth.

    (B) are overemphasized.

    (C) need to be reformed.

    (D) are worthwhile endeavors.

    (E) create a sense of camaraderie among students.

Directions: *For questions 28–38, select the lettered choice most nearly opposite in meaning to the word given in CAPITAL letters. Circle the letter of your choice.*

---

28. HYPERBOLE:

    (A) overstatement

    (B) hypnotism

    (C) deemphasis

    (D) rhythm

    (E) stanza

29. EXTEMPORANEOUS:
    (A) fastidious
    (B) prepared
    (C) contemporaneous
    (D) informal
    (E) informed

30. FACETIOUS:
    (A) flippant
    (B) facile
    (C) gratuitous
    (D) grave
    (E) fractious

31. POLEMIC:
    (A) kudos
    (B) persiflage
    (C) anathema
    (D) rubric
    (E) platitude

32. UNDAUNTED:
    (A) dauntless
    (B) remiss
    (C) amiss
    (D) intimated
    (E) dispirited

33. ALACRITY:
    (A) elasticity
    (B) finality
    (C) intervention
    (D) procrastination
    (E) hypocrisy

34. TRADUCE:
    (A) defend
    (B) defray
    (C) betray
    (D) bewilder
    (E) detract

35. GRANDILOQUENT:
    (A) euphuistic
    (B) aphonic
    (C) cryptic
    (D) euphonic
    (E) reticent

36. ACCRETION:
    (A) secretion
    (B) reparation
    (C) agglomeration
    (D) dearth
    (E) contrition

37. VISCERAL:
    (A) vertiginous
    (B) impalpable
    (C) virulent
    (D) impeccable
    (E) incorporeal

38. PROPINQUITY:
    (A) confluence
    (B) resonance
    (C) perspicacity
    (D) iniquity
    (E) distance

Quick Answer Guide

Test 1, Part 5: Verbal (2)

1. A	11. D	21. C	31. A
2. D	12. D	22. D	32. E
3. E	13. D	23. E	33. D
4. C	14. B	24. A	34. A
5. B	15. B	25. B	35. E
6. A	16. D	26. C	36. D
7. A	17. D	27. D	37. E
8. C	18. B	28. C	38. E
9. C	19. C	29. B	
10. E	20. C	30. D	

For explanations to these questions, see Day 20.

Day 20

Test 1, Part 5: Verbal (2).

Explanations and Strategies

Assignment for Today:

Review the explanations for the Verbal Test you took on Day 19.

---

1. The correct answer is (A). accessible

Flag words: "instead of." The correct choice will mean the opposite of *erudite*, which means scholarly, educated. *Accessible* means simple or understandable. This would describe what the president is trying to do with her simple examples and common words.

The president's speech contained common words and simple examples because her advisers counseled her to be more *accessible* instead of being so erudite.

2. The correct answer is (D). punished

Reading through the sentence should give you some idea of which word will fill in the blank. The sentence describes a medieval attitude toward heresy. Heresy is religious dissent or disobedience. You can probably guess that the attitude is not positive. Choice (D) fits well. Heretics were *punished*.

Soon after Mary ascended the English throne in 1553, Parliament voted to reinstate the medieval law that *punished* heresy by burning at the stake.

3. The correct answer is (E). announced..elect

The best way to find the missing words is to read the sentence and anticipate the choices. Because the sentence describes actions taking place during a political convention, you can expect to find words that relate to politics. The first blank should have a word like "said"; both *indicated* and *announced* work well. The word "select" would fit well in the second blank; of the choices given, *elect* works best.

During the final meeting of the convention, the chairperson *announced* that nominations to *elect* a party candidate would begin.

4. The correct answer is (C). ephemeral

Ephemeral, or short-lived, is the best answer here. If the medalist's fame has died before she even gets home, that's pretty short.

The Olympic gold medalist found that her fame was *ephemeral* because by the time she arrived home, no one even remembered what she had achieved.

5. The correct answer is (B). analyzed..disciplined

Your best approach here is to read the choices and eliminate the ones that don't make sense. In doing this, you'll find that choice (B) works well, much better than the other choices.

The Sophists taught that influencing forces can be *analyzed* systematically and can be understood through the use of a *disciplined* mind.

6. The correct answer is (A). pious..expurgated

Reading through the choices is the best way to find the right words. The important thing is to find a word pair that fits the overall meaning of the sentence. Choice (A) turns out to be the best answer. *Pious* means earnestly religious. To *expurgate* is to cut out material. These two words make sense together and with the rest of the sentence.

The owner of the small-town movie theater was a *pious* man who regularly *expurgated* films he thought would be objectionable to his conservative clientele.

7. The correct answer is (A). penchant..ingrained

There's a flag: "but." However, it's still a complicated sentence requiring context clues. So, start with the second blank first. Try to understand the sentence's meaning: What is characteristic of the village architect? It's the *automatic habit* of setting aside space for an outhouse. (An outhouse is an outside restroom or lavatory.) Something automatic must be deeply fixed. That's *ingrained*, which means "firmly fixed or deeply rooted."

Penchant means "strong inclination or liking." Plug in both. Makes sense, doesn't it?

The clearest symbol of the village architect is not a *penchant* for a simple facade but the automatic allocation of space for an outhouse that stems from a long and deeply *ingrained* way of life.

8. The correct answer is (C). mentor:guide

truck—a motor vehicle used for hauling things.
haul—to transport.

A *truck* is used in order to *haul*.

To find the right answer, you need to see that hauling is the defining characteristic of a truck. Here's a sentence that can help you determine the right answer: If it can't haul, it can't be defined as a truck.

Is a *mentor* used in order to *guide*? Yes. In fact, the defining characteristic of *mentor* is that he or she is a *guide*, just as the defining characteristic of a *truck* is that it can *haul*.

9. The correct answer is (C). drought:rain

famine—lack of food.
food—something you eat.

A *famine* is a lack of *food*.

Is a *drought* the lack of *rain*? Yes, so *drought* has the same relationship to *rain* as *famine* does to *food*.

10. The correct answer is (E). baker:bread

vintner—someone who makes wine.
wine—alcoholic beverage made from grapes.

A *vintner* is someone who makes *wine*.

Does a *baker* make *bread*? Yes! Therefore, *vintner* is to *wine* as *baker* is to *bread*.

11. The correct answer is (D). frontier:pioneer

space—the expanse where the solar system and beyond exist.
cosmonaut—a Russian astronaut, someone who travels through space.

A *cosmonaut* is someone who travels through *space*.

Is a *pioneer* someone who travels through a *frontier*? A *frontier* is an unexplored territory. A pioneer might travel through a frontier, exploring it just as a cosmonaut explores space. So, this is the right answer: *space* is to *cosmonaut* as *frontier* is to *pioneer*.

12. The correct answer is (D). atelier:artistry

office—a room or set of rooms in which business is transacted.

metier—a skilled trade; a craft or expertise.

An *office* is one place where a person can conduct his or her *metier*.

Is an *atelier* a place where a person can conduct his or her *artistry*? Yes. An *atelier* is a workshop or artist's studio.

13. The correct answer is (D). moratorium:repayment

tourniquet—a device that halts the flow of blood.

blood—fluid circulating in the vertebrate vascular system.

A *tourniquet* halts the flow of *blood*.

Does a *moratorium* halt or arrest *repayment*? Yes. A *moratorium* is a legally authorized delay in an action or the payment of a debt.

14. The correct answer is (B). materialistic:bourgeois

promiscuous—indiscriminate in choice of sexual partners.

harlot—a lewd woman, a prostitute.

A *harlot* is *promiscuous*.

Is the *bourgeois* materialistic? The *bourgeois* is middle-class: wrapped up in *materialistic* concerns, ruled by property values, or lacking in artistic taste. Is it characteristic for the *bourgeois* to be *materialistic*? Typically, yes. A tough one.

15. The correct answer is (B). saturated:solution

plenary—full, complete.

assembly—a formal gathering or meeting.

A *plenary assembly* is an *assembly* attended by all members. It is a full or complete *assembly*.

Is a *saturated solution* full or complete? A *saturated solution* contains the greatest amount of material that can be dissolved in it.

16. The correct answer is (D). circumlocutory:terse

circumspect—careful or proper.

indecorous—not careful or improper.

Circumspect means nearly the opposite of *indecorous*.

Does *circumlocutory* mean nearly the opposite of *terse*? Yes. *Circumlocutory* means using lots of words. *Terse* means using few words. Therefore, *circumspect* is to *indecorous* as *circumlocutory* is to *terse*. Yes, this was a tough one.

17. The correct answer is (D).

Throughout the passage, the author extols the virtues of Whitman's writing. In the first paragraph, the author tells us that Whitman was one of the "voices of the earth," who spoke with a voice "as authentic as the hills."

18. The correct answer is (B).

The passage, largely a celebration of Whitman's writing, could thus be called "laudatory," which means relating to or expressing praise.

19. The correct answer is (C).

In the first paragraph, the author tells us that Whitman "left nothing out" of his writing, and in the last paragraph, we are told that his life was "a mixture of lawful and lawless propensities" and that "certain of his vices are indecent." The implication is that Whitman wrote about life as he saw it and that what he saw might make more than a few readers blush.

20. The correct answer is (C).

What in the world is "bathybius"? Look at what follows this word. The protoplasm-like virtues of Whitman: "poems in solution," "crystallizable," and "waiting for structural change." Protoplasm is not settled. It's always moving, taking on a different shape. So, a choice that reflects such a changeable and unsettled quality would be a possible meaning.

Something constantly changing would likely be uncategorizable.

21. The correct answer is (C).

This passage is a book review, plain and simple. Even though the first three paragraphs make no mention of a book, the fourth paragraph makes it clear that the author is responding to a book recently written by Mr. Keppel. The fifth paragraph continues the review by outlining the book, topic by topic. Of course, along the way, the author of the passage also gets a few words in about education.

22. The correct answer is (D).

Paragraph one contains a list of accusations about undergraduate colleges. All of the responses listed are in paragraph one except choice (D), disregard for student needs. Therefore, this is the right answer.

23. The correct answer is (E).

In the context of the sentence, the best meaning for "dubious" is "questionable." The author is saying that colleges have been accused of providing opportunities for falsified and questionable research— questionable meaning both in truthfulness and in value.

24. The correct answer is (A).

Paragraph two compares a university to a number of other institutions, including a church. The point is that all these institutions require "outside irritation" before they change. The university, the author says, is no different. Therefore, outside criticism often leads to change.

25. The correct answer is (B).

In paragraph three, the author is saying that all the colleges are changing rapidly but that the better institutions have changed more. The author describes the change as a "little less than a revolution," which is quite drastic.

26. The correct answer is (C).

Paragraph four lists Keppel's qualification to write a book on undergraduate institutions. Check which choice is *not* mentioned in the passage. If you are careful, you'll find that the words in choice (C) are men-

tioned ("evolution" and "present stages"), but they are not used in the same sense as in choice (C). Therefore, choice (C) is the one that is not mentioned.

27. The correct answer is (D).

The correct answer to this question is not immediately clear; you have to find the answer by finding its opposite. In the last paragraph, the author states that some people are against intercollegiate athletics, but *not* Mr. Keppel. From this, we can safely infer that Mr. Keppel feels athletic programs are worthwhile.

28. The correct answer is (C). deemphasis

Hyperbole means overstatement.

　　Deemphasis means understatement. Is *deemphasis* the opposite of *hyperbole*? Yes—one means understatement, the other overstatement.

29. The correct answer is (B). prepared

Extemporaneous means impromptu, at the spur of the moment, not planned.

　　Prepared means planned in advance. Is *prepared* the opposite of *extemporaneous*? An impromptu speech would not be planned in advance.

30. The correct answer is (D). grave

Facetious means not serious.

　　Grave means somber, serious. Is *grave* the opposite of *facetious*? Yes, *grave* means somber or very serious, the opposite of *facetious*, which means not serious.

31. The correct answer is (A). kudos

Polemic means an attack on the principles of another.

　　Kudos means praise. Is *kudos* the opposite of *polemic*? Yes, at least given the other choices.

32. The correct answer is (E). dispirited

Undaunted means not discouraged.

　　Dispirited means deprived of enthusiasm. Is *dispirited* the opposite of *undaunted*? Yes, whereas a *dispirited* person would be discouraged, or deprived of enthusiasm, an *undaunted* person would be enthusiastic despite possible obstacles.

33. The correct answer is (D). procrastination

Alacrity means prompt response.

  Procrastination means to put off (delay) intentionally and habitually. Is *procrastination* the opposite of *alacrity*? Yes, to put off intentionally and habitually is not a prompt response.

34. The correct answer is (A). defend

Traduce means malign, to make malicious statements.

  Defend means to ward off attack. Is *defend* the opposite of *traduce*? Yes, one word is defensive, the other offensive.

35. The correct answer is (E). reticent

Grandiloquent means a lofty or pompous speaking style.

  Reticent means restrained in expression. Is *reticent* the opposite of *grandiloquent*? Yes, a grandiloquent speaking style is the opposite of a restrained style of expression.

36. The correct answer is (D). dearth

Accretion means accumulation, adding up.

  Dearth means an inadequate supply. Is *dearth* the opposite of *accretion*? Yes, if you accumulate something, you probably have a lot of it, which is the opposite of *dearth*, not having enough of something.

37. The correct answer is (E). incorporeal

Visceral means bodily or corporeal.

  Incorporeal means having no material body or form. Is *incorporeal* the opposite of *visceral*? Yes, *incorporeal* and corporeal (*visceral*) are opposites.

38. The correct answer is (E). distance

Propinquity means nearness.

  Distance means degree or amount of separation. Is *distance* the opposite of *propinquity*? Yes, the two words have opposite meanings.

Test 1, Parts 6A and 6B:
Issue Essay and Argument Analysis

Sample Topic

Assignment for Today:

Write an issue essay and an argument analysis on the given topics.

For the following exercise, we recommend that you set aside 75 minutes of uninterrupted time (45 minutes for the issue essay and 30 minutes for the argument analysis). Clear your desk, except for some scratch paper and a stop watch, and take this test under real test-like conditions.

ISSUE ESSAY

Present your perspective on the issue below, using relevant reasons and/or examples to support your views. Time limit: 45 minutes.

"Contemporary media focus on fragmented information and neglect thematic issues that cut across stories. Most of the news segments on television are no longer than 2 minutes in length. As a result, people tend to think only in terms of discrete events, without paying attention to how the various events connect with each other."

ARGUMENT ANALYSIS ESSAY

Discuss how well reasoned you find this argument. Time limit: 30 minutes.

The following appeared in an article published in the *Daily American* newspaper.

"Our citizens are getting more and more obese, as revealed by a number of studies that have tracked the body mass index of Americans over the last six decades. Some researchers attribute this to television, computers, and video games. The elderly population is watching more television, middle-age people are spending more time in front of their computers, and the young are playing video games. All of these activities, some experts believe, contribute to a lack of physical activity, which results in increased obesity. Some studies have shown, however, that in regions of the country with milder climates, obesity levels are lower than in regions with harsher climates. These latter studies attribute a lack of opportunity to exercise outdoors as a primary determinant of obesity."

Test 1, Parts 6A and 6B:
Issue Essay and Argument Analysis
Sample Essay Responses

Assignment for Today:

Analyze your issue essay and argument analysis from Day 21.

ISSUE ESSAY EXAMPLE

As mentioned previously, the best way to analyze your essay is to show it to others and ask for their feedback. So, do not forget to do so.

Here are some strategies that we hope you used before writing your paper.

"Contemporary media focus on fragmented information and neglect thematic issues that cut across stories. Most of the news segments on television are no longer than 2 minutes in length. As a result, people tend to think only in terms of discrete events, without paying attention to how the various events connect with each other."

You need to first decide whether you will support, oppose, present a qualified support, or question the assumptions.

Your position (underline one or more):

Support	Oppose	Qualified support	Question assumption

Then, write down the points that you will make.

1. _____
2. _____
3. _____
4. _____
5. _____

Here is an example:

Support	Oppose	Qualified support	Question assumption

1. Definition of contemporary media is too narrow.
2. Exposure = thinking
3. People do not assimilate the information on their own.
4. Stories: examples of how information gets assimilated
5. Conditional agreement
6. Implications of the passage, if true

Sample Essay

While your essay will be quite different, compare it with the sample below in terms of approach, structure, and execution.

The given passage is supposedly about "contemporary" media, but it seems to be limited only to television news. There are lots of other forms of media in contemporary society that people use to get their information. Examples of these kinds of media include the Internet, newspapers, and magazines. Hence, the author of the passage needs to limit the claim to only television news. Even if the passage were limited to discussing the effects of television news, its claims are too broad.

The passage also seems to assume that there will be a one-to-one correlation between the content of television news and people's thinking styles. It's one thing to say that, after repeated exposure to discrete news stories on television, people will believe that such events are not connected with each other in the real world. It's quite another to claim that people's thinking will follow the same pattern. Surely people make a distinction between news, as they observe it on television, and events that occur in their daily lives.

The passage is also based on the premise that, just because television news presents events as unconnected with each other, people do not assimilate the many small pieces of information into a coherent story. It is likely that people have become quite sophisticated in their ability to integrate information and identify hidden patterns.

Powerful stories, it can be argued, are examples of the integration of fragmented information. If the claim in the passage were true, we should see fewer and less powerful stories circulating in contemporary society. Yet, judging from the success of bestsellers and Hollywood films, one can hardly reach this conclusion. If anything, the logical conclusion seems to be that we have more stories today than at any time in the past.

There is no question that some media present information as discrete fragments. And we can expand the concept of "media" to include other means of disseminating information. An example is Power Point, the popular software used to make presentations. This technology forces the user to synthesize complex ideas into bullet points. If the author of the passage is correct, over time, the users of Power Point and those who consume such presentations may lose the ability to connect the points and see the bigger picture. If this happens, it may help to prove the author's point.

ARGUMENT ANALYSIS EXAMPLE

"Our citizens are getting more and more obese, as revealed by a number of studies that have tracked the body mass index of Americans over the last six decades. Some researchers attribute this to television, computers, and video games. The elderly population is watching more television, middle-age people are spending more time in front of their computers, and the young are playing video games. All of these activities, some experts believe, contribute to a lack of physical activity, which results in increased obesity. Some studies have shown, however, that in regions of the country with milder climates, obesity levels are lower than in regions with harsher climates. These latter studies attribute a lack of opportunity to exercise outdoors as a primary determinant of obesity."

First, if you didn't already, make a list of assumptions and/or conclusions that you can spot in the given argument.

Assumption 1: _____

Assumption 2: _____

Assumption 3: _____

Conclusion 1: _____

Conclusion 2: _____

Then decide which of the arguments and conclusions you are going to attack or support and elaborate. Your list may look something like this:

Assumption 1: Only lack of physical activity causes obesity.

Assumption 2: Role of fast food outlets doesn't matter.

Assumption 3: Genetics don't matter.

Assumption 4: Across the board, everyone is getting more obese.

Conclusion: Partial support for the claim

Given that we have now identified some of the underlying assumptions, we are ready to begin writing the essay. Here is a sample. Compare your essay with this one in terms of approach, structure, and execution.

One of the central problems with this passage is its assumption that obesity is the result of only one cause—lack of physical activity. There is little doubt that when people do not engage in physical activity, their metabolism slows down and they begin to store more fat in their tissues. There are, however, other significant causes of obesity that the passage seems to neglect. Diet is one such factor. By framing the obesity issue exclusively in terms of physical activity, the passage's underlying assumption is that people's dietary practices have remained unchanged. Could it be the case that people are now consuming more fatty foods than at any time in the past? Even though I do not know how many fast-food outlets there are today, per capita, compared with the number over the last six decades, I have observed many such establishments in my neighborhood. Given that I live in a fairly typical American town, I assume that the same is happening elsewhere.

I have also read elsewhere that we are spending more time at work than at any time in our history. If this is true, it is logical to assume that people have less time to prepare meals at home, which means that many more people are probably eating out these days than in the past. Hence, it is entirely possible that the increase we have seen in obesity can be attributed to two factors: more fast-food outlets and less time to cook and eat at home.

The passage also seems to disregard the powerful role of genetics in determining obesity. If it is true that we are getting increasingly more obese, it may be that we are transmitting the "fat" gene from one generation to another. Hence, today's children may be fat not because they are less physically active, but because they have inherited the fat gene from their parents through a mechanism that selects for that trait.

The passage does not make a distinction between obese and healthier individuals. If we look at magazine racks in bookstores these days, we see more and more magazines dedicated to staying healthy, running, and engaging in other outdoor activities. This indicates to me that a sizable population is concerned about physical health. There are more soccer players in the United States today than at any time in the past. There are also more marathon runners, swimmers, and other sports enthusiasts. This would indicate that a certain segment of the population does engage in physical activity. By not making this distinction, the passage leaves the reader with the impression that everyone is getting more obese.

All this being said, I do not have a problem accepting the claim that, across the population, our average obesity rates have been increasing. My primary objection is with the implied claim in the passage that this rise in obesity can be attributed solely to people's patterns of physical activity. By neglecting other sources of obesity, we seem to be giving these sources a free pass.

Day 23 to **Day 30**

TEST 2

Questions and Answers

Explanations and Strategies

Test 2, Part 1: Math (1).

Questions and Answers

Assignment for Today:

Take the first part of a practice GRE Math Test under actual test conditions. Allow yourself exactly 30 minutes to complete all 30 questions in this test.

Directions: *For questions 1–15, each question contains two quantities—one on the left (Column A) and one on the right (Column B). Compare the quantities and answer*

(A) if Column A is greater than Column B

(B) if Column B is greater than Column A

(C) if the two columns are equal

(D) if you cannot determine a definite relationship from the information given

Never answer (E)

In some questions, information appears centered between the two columns. Centered information concerns each of the columns for that question only. Any symbol in one column represents the same value if it appears in the other column.

Column A	Column B

$$\frac{12x}{5} = \frac{3}{y}$$

1. | 5 | $4xy$ |

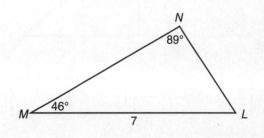

2. | *MN* | *NL* |

Column A	Column B

$$y^5 - y^5 = 0$$

$$xy \neq 0$$

3.

$\dfrac{x^2}{y^4}$	$\dfrac{1}{xy}$

Let $\langle u|v|w \rangle = \dfrac{u}{v} + \dfrac{v}{w}$, where u, v, and w are integers, and $v \neq 0$ and $w \neq 0$.

4.

$\langle 4|-2|-1 \rangle$	0

$$-7 \leq y < 4$$

5.

The greatest possible value of $-8y$	The greatest possible value of $14y$

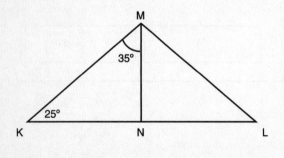

6.

KN	NL

Column A	Column B

Clyde's bicycle has wheels of radius 8 inches. Donna's bicycle has wheels of radius 16 inches. During a race, each wheel of Clyde's bicycle turns 60 times per minute, and each wheel of Donna's bicycle turns 30 times per minute.

7.

The distance traveled by Clyde's bicycle every minute	The distance traveled by Donna's bicycle every minute

In December, a $100 sweater was discounted 20%. In April, the sweater was placed on a clearance rack and the discounted price was cut in half.

8.

Total price of the sweater in April, including a 6% sales tax	$46

$$x > y > 0$$

9.

$\left(7\dfrac{x}{y}\right)^2 + \left(2\dfrac{x}{y}\right)^2$	$\left(9\dfrac{x}{y}\right)^2$

Column A	Column B

g is an even integer, and $16 \le g \le 20$.

h is an odd integer, and $5 \le h \le 15$.

$$g = 2h$$

10.	$g + h$	27

---

k is a negative integer

11.	$\dfrac{1}{k^5 + k^3}$	$\dfrac{1}{k^5}$

Let the operation # have the property that $x \# y = -(y \# x)$ for all real numbers x and y.

12.	$1 \# 2$	$2 \# 1$

$$q = \dfrac{8}{9}$$

13.	$q^2 + q^4 + q^6$	$q + q^3 + q^5$

Column A	Column B

The product of three consecutive *odd* integers is 15 times their sum.

14.	The average (arithmetic mean) of the three integers	9

For all positive numbers c,

$$\langle\langle c \rangle\rangle = \dfrac{c}{2} + \dfrac{1}{2} \quad \text{if } c \ge 3$$

$$\langle\langle c \rangle\rangle = c + 1 \quad \text{if } c < 3$$

15.	$\langle\langle 6 - 2 \rangle\rangle$	$\langle\langle 6 \rangle\rangle - \langle\langle 2 \rangle\rangle$

Directions: For questions 16–30, solve each problem, and circle the appropriate answer choice, A–E.

16. If y is an unknown and $10,105 + y = 12,125$, then what is the value of $10,105 - 5y$?

   (A)   5
   (B)   2,020
   (C)   8,085
   (D)   10,100
   (E)   20,205

17. If u, v, w, and x are odd integers between 5 and 11 inclusive, and $u < v < w < x$, which of the following is an odd integer?

   (A) $\dfrac{(u+v+w+x)}{4}$
   (B) $(u)\,(v)\,(w)\,(x)$
   (C) $(v-u)\,(x-w)$
   (D) $(u-v)\,(w-x)$
   (E) $\dfrac{(u+v)}{2} + \dfrac{(w+x)}{2}$

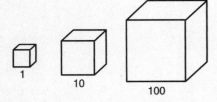

Note: Figure not drawn to scale.

18. What is the sum of the total surface areas of the three cubes shown above if the given dimensions represent the length of each edge of the cube?

   (A)   666
   (B)   10,101
   (C)   60,066
   (D)   60,606
   (E)   1,001,001

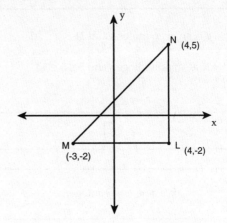

19. In the figure above, what is the length of MN?

   (A) $\sqrt{10}$
   (B) $\sqrt{98}$
   (C)   14
   (D) $\dfrac{49}{2}$
   (E)   98

20. If the diameter of a planet's circular orbit is about 1.28×10^4 meters, what is the approximate area, in square meters, of the circle enclosed by the orbit?

   (A) $0.4 \times 10^4\,\pi$
   (B) $1.4 \times 10^4\,\pi$
   (C) $0.4 \times 10^6\,\pi$
   (D) $0.4 \times 10^8\,\pi$
   (E) $1.4 \times 10^8\,\pi$

Questions 21–25 are based on the following figure.

```
        Students in Jefferson High School's
                  Class of 1996
          Total number of students: 872

Males                                    Females
(468)                                     (404)
_____

                    Ethnicity

219               Anglo-Saxon               187
 86               Asian                      63
 97               Black                      107
 59               Hispanic                   44
  2               Native American             0
  5               Other                       3


              Number of Awards Won

 48                    4                     58
127                    3                    154
189                    2                    122
 92                    1                     68
 12                    0                      4


              Post-High School Plans

234               College-bound             287
149               Work-bound                 83
 85               Undecided                  34
```

NOTE: The following categories are listed by the approximate _percent_ of students participating in each activity by gender. Percentage figures don't necessarily add up to 100.

```
               Sports Participation

13                Football                   0
 7                Soccer                     4
20                Track & Field             20
20                Swimming                   5
 8                Tennis                     7


                Club Participation

 9                Science Club               6
17                Languages                 18
 3                Glee Club                  7
23                Drama Club                21
 6                Math Club                  3
 8                Debate Team                8
```

21. How many students are undecided about their post-high school plans?

    (A) 34

    (B) 51

    (C) 85

    (D) 119

    (E) 129

22. Approximately how many students participate in swimming?

    (A) 20

    (B) 25

    (C) 94

    (D) 114

    (E) 218

23. If all of the Hispanic students in the school participate in track & field, approximately how many non-Hispanic students participate in track & field?

    (A) 35

    (B) 37

    (C) 72

    (D) 103

    (E) 175

24. What is the average number of awards won by female students?

    (A) Between 0 and 1

    (B) Between 1 and 2

    (C) Between 2 and 3

    (D) Between 3 and 4

    (E) It cannot be determined.

25. Which of the following statements can be inferred from the data given?

    I. The percent of male students who are undecided about their post-high school plans is greater than the percentage of work-bound female students.

    II. More than 50 percent of the students in Jefferson High School's Class of 1996 are males.

    III. An equal number of male and female students participate in the debate team.

    (A) I only

    (B) II only

    (C) III only

    (D) I and II

    (E) I, II, and III

26. The sum of 12 numbers is 276. If 4 numbers are removed, the average (arithmetic mean) of the remaining numbers is 26. What is the average of the four numbers removed?

    (A) 17

    (B) 26

    (C) 43

    (D) 68

    (E) 104

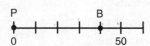

27. The tick marks in the figure above are equally spaced.

    If line segment *AB* is 30% longer than line segment *PB*, which of the following could be the value of *A*?

    (A) 12

    (B) 52

    (C) 62

    (D) 92

    (E) 102

28. Two trains travel without stopping from station A to station B, a distance of 480 miles. The first train travels at 40 miles per hour, and the second train travels at 120 miles per hour. If the first train leaves station A at 11:00 a.m., at what time must the second train leave station A in order to arrive at station B at the exact time that the first train arrives?

    (A) 2:00 p.m.

    (B) 3:00 p.m.

    (C) 7:00 p.m.

    (D) 8:00 p.m.

    (E) 11:00 p.m.

29. A trip from town W to town Z must go through towns X and Y. If the distance between towns W and X is $\frac{1}{4}$ larger than the average distance of the three trip segments, and the distance between towns W and Y is $\frac{5}{6}$ of the total distance between towns W and Z, what is the ratio of the distance between X and Y to the distance between Y and Z?

    (A) 1:2

    (B) 3:2

    (C) 5:2

    (D) 5:72

    (E) 10:7

30. A certain hockey player scored 1 goal per game in the first two games. In every other game in which he played, he scored *at least* four goals per game. If his overall average (arithmetic mean) is exactly three goals per game, what is the *most* number of games he could have played?

    (A) 4

    (B) 5

    (C) 6

    (D) 7

    (E) It cannot be determined from the information given.

Quick Answer Guide

Test 2, Part 1: Math (1)

1. C	9. B	17. B	25. B
2. B	10. C	18. D	26. A
3. C	11. A	19. B	27. D
4. C	12. D	20. D	28. C
5. A	13. B	21. D	29. C
6. D	14. B	22. D	30. C
7. C	15. A	23. C	
8. B	16. A	24. C	

For explanations of these questions, see Day 25.

Test 2, Part 2: Verbal (1).

Questions and Answers

Assignment for Today:

Take the first part of a practice GRE Verbal Test under actual test conditions. Allow yourself exactly 30 minutes to complete the 38 questions in this test.

Directions: *For questions 1–7, one or more words have been left out of each sentence. Circle the answer, A–E, that contains the word or words that best fit the meaning of the entire sentence.*

---

1. Because the cyberware industry was just beginning to boom, Olivia's small technology company grew rapidly and quickly became ____.
   - (A) obsequious
   - (B) indigent
   - (C) lucrative
   - (D) voluble
   - (E) exotic

2. Even though Brian was unattractive and ____, whenever he talked on the phone, he acted as though he were the most ____ and outgoing man in the world.
   - (A) retiring..handsome
   - (B) dull..frivolous
   - (C) depraved..diligent
   - (D) poor..disagreeable
   - (E) suave..bereft

3. The newborn's incessant wailing convinced the young mother that it was impossible to ____ her ____ infant.
   - (A) dominate..unruly
   - (B) placate..discontented
   - (C) satisfy..empathetic
   - (D) delude..colicky
   - (E) enthrall..indolent

4. The meaning of the original Egyptian "picture writing" remains a mystery to modern civilizations long after these ancient hieroglyphics have been ____.
   - (A) defaced
   - (B) decanted
   - (C) deciphered
   - (D) debunked
   - (E) debriefed

5. Every night, the artist would lock herself in her ____ and work ____ to finish all her paintings in time for her exhibition.

   (A) studio..sporadically

   (B) chateau..somberly

   (C) retreat..perilously

   (D) bedroom..industriously

   (E) atelier..assiduously

6. A(n) ____ essay, Marcel Mauss' *The Gift*, is acknowledged by many as having created the field of economic anthropology.

   (A) parochial

   (B) apocryphal

   (C) jejune

   (D) seminal

   (E) eponymous

7. While many think of advertisements as being uniformly ____ and ____ , some of the most shocking and disturbing pictures in the media may be found in ads.

   (A) anodyne..idyllic

   (B) subliminal..erotic

   (C) misleading..manipulative

   (D) contrived..unimaginative

   (E) innovative..inspiring

Directions: *For questions 8–16, determine the relationship between the two words given in capital letters. Then, from the choices listed A–E, select the one pair that has a relationship most similar to that of the capitalized pair. Circle the letter of that pair.*

---

8. SMOKE:CONFLAGRATION::

   (A) breathing:exercise

   (B) exhaust:pipe

   (C) moisture:precipitation

   (D) gravity:attraction

   (E) light:reflection

9. BULWARK:PRIVACY::

   (A) mailbox:communication

   (B) jail:sanctuary

   (C) village:activity

   (D) spy:danger

   (E) jacket:warmth

10. GRAVITY:MIRTH::

    (A) levity:laughter

    (B) fealty:oath

    (C) energy:force

    (D) inertia:fatigue

    (E) sincerity:guile

11. GARRULOUS:LACONIC::

    (A) succulent:juicy

    (B) weighty:pithy

    (C) placid:proud

    (D) bombastic:demure

    (E) onerous:noisome

12. FLATTERY:SYCOPHANCY::

    (A) modesty:arrogance

    (B) spleen:generosity

    (C) invective:honesty

    (D) malice:animosity

    (E) clarity:obscurity

13. CAR:BRAKE::

    (A) war:treaty

    (B) ship:sailor

    (C) flu:inoculation

    (D) mileage:transmission

    (E) conception:birth

14. PARLAY:TRANSFORM::

    (A) recount:redound

    (B) overwhelm:surrender

    (C) disabuse:mistake

    (D) discern:confuse

    (E) eclipse:surpass

15. PLIANT:OBDURATE::

    (A) insensible:ingenious

    (B) malleable:flaccid

    (C) silent:nocturnal

    (D) predatory:carnivorous

    (E) glowing:flaming

16. TINY:HOMUNCULUS::

    (A) dead:corpse

    (B) still:lake

    (C) immense:shoe

    (D) dangerous:animal

    (E) teenage:girl

Directions: *Read each passage and answer the questions that follow. Base your answers only on what is stated or implied in the passage.*

Questions 17–20 are based on the following passage.

The pearl, so highly valued for its chaste beauty, is but a secretion of animal matter, resulting from the efforts of some uneasy mollusk, annoyed by a foreign substance, which has found its way
(5) into his habitation, to make the best of an unavoidable evil by enclosing it in a soft, smooth covering. Let us imitate the oyster; when annoyed or afflicted, by meekness and patience strive to turn our vexations and troubles into
(10) "pearls of great price," valuable products of beauty and wonder.

It is on the northwest coast of the island of Ceylon, in the Indian Ocean, that the pearl oyster most abounds, and there it is that the pearl
(15) fishery is conducted in the most extensive, systematic, and successful manner. A single oyster will sometimes contain several pearls, which are generally embedded in the body of the animal, but are sometimes fixed to the shell. It is re-
(20) corded of one rich oyster that there were found in his possession no less than 150 precious jewels. He must have been a miser, or perhaps he had taken them in pledge from his less provident neighbors.

(25) From the earliest times, pearls have been considered to be valuable ornaments, and are often alluded to by Greek and Roman writers. Various attempts have been made to imitate them, and one mode of producing them, practiced, it is
(30) said, more than a thousand years ago, is still carried on in China. In the shells of pearl oysters, holes are bored, into which pieces of iron are introduced; these wounding and irritating the animal, cause it to deposit coat upon coat of
(35) pearly matter over the wounded part, and so the pearl is formed. Artificial pearls are made of hollow glass globules or little gloves, covered on the inside with a liquid called pearl-essence, and filled up with white wax. Historians speak of an
(40) ancient traffic in native pearls carried on in Great Britain. Generally, artificially produced pearls are inferior in the two requisites of color and size.

Native divers who subsist on their finding these "gems" expose themselves to danger from
(45) voracious sharks, which hover about the fishing grounds, and make a dash at their victim, heedless of the written charms with which the shark-charmer has provided him previous to his descent. The diver, upon retrieving a day's worth
(50) of work, places the fruits of his labor in heaps, where they are allowed to remain until they become putrid, at which time they undergo a very elaborate process of washing and separating from the shells, which are carefully examined
(55) and deprived from their pearly treasures. The stench arising from the decomposed animal matter is described as horrible, and the whole process is filthy and loathsome. Yet out of the slime and mud and disgusting effluvia come
(60) gems of inestimable value, calculated to adorn the brow of beauty and form ornaments the most pure and delicate that can be imagined.

17. The main purpose of the passage is to

    (A) teach the reader how to find natural pearls and create artificial ones.

    (B) explain why pearls are valuable.

    (C) compare artificial pearls with natural pearls.

    (D) argue that pearls are among the most interesting gems found in nature.

    (E) explain bits of the history, hunting, and production of pearls.

18. In comparing artificial and natural pearls, the author of the passage implies that

    (A) Ceylon produces most of the world's artificial pearls.

    (B) artificial pearls result from irritants, while natural pearls do not.

    (C) natural pearls are larger and more beautiful than artificial pearls.

    (D) artificial pearls will survive longer than natural ones.

    (E) natural pearls were in great demand in China.

19. In describing how artificial pearls are made, the passage indicates all of the following steps EXCEPT

    (A) fill the globule with white wax.

    (B) use a liquid called pearl-essence.

    (C) start with hollow glass globules.

    (D) introduce an iron pellet.

    (E) fill a "little glove" with liquid.

20. One can infer from the passage that an irony of a pearl's beauty is that

    (A) people can make pearls just as beautiful.

    (B) pearls have not been in big demand recently.

    (C) collecting pearls is a stinky business.

    (D) some oysters contain no pearls at all.

    (E) something natural can cost so much.

Questions 21–27 are based on the following passage.

The word "kitchenette" seems admirably descriptive, for it really tells you what it is, a little kitchen; whereas, a suffragette is not a little suffrage, nor Hamlet a little ham. One warms up to
(5) kitchenette, the word, before one is warmed up by kitchenette, the thing.

The idea of a tiny place where you can handily reach everything you need in the preparation and serving of food is truly fascinating. On your
(10) right is the refrigerator, on your left the sink, just above are pots and pans. Open a drawer and lo, you have your forks and spoons and other table utilities—all actually without moving. It is almost beyond belief how convenient it is. The
(15) water runs hot or cold, and the microwave is right at eye level for speed cooking. It is all a miracle of condensation and comfort. After a careful calculation—this is a most conservative estimate—I am ready to declare that in the use
(20) of a kitchenette, you save in steps no less than three miles a day over an ordinary good-sized kitchen.

A notable asset of the kitchenette is the superb way in which you become by means of it
(25) independent of help. A mere individual with any knack at all for boiling an egg and making a cup of coffee can, with the assistance of that urban lifesaver, the delicatessen, have a breakfast a king could not outdo. When you stop to think of it,
(30) what could or would any sovereign have for his matutinal meal more than you, kitchenetted and fearless, can provide? Fruit, cereal, fresh cream, the egg done to a turn (this does not seem quite the correct idiom, but let it pass), coffee that
(35) smokes its fragrant way to heaven, and crisp rolls with their dab of dainty butter; yes, and, be it whispered, sugar enough not to make the berry brown and beloved a mockery; what more could any mortal, be one queen or king, desire
(40) here below? Merely to enumerate the items of such a breakfast makes me hungry. And this delectable result is easy to manage because the kitchenette has come in these latter days to simplify, to soothe, and to sanctify these homely,
(45) necessary details of daily living.

But we have hardly more than begun to cata-
logue the virtues of our kitchenette. If it has been
implied that breakfast is the only meal to be got
in the kitchenette, an injustice has been done to
(50) ourselves, and the subject. Not so. Even the un-
skilled hand can evoke dishes that are not only
suitable for lunch but welcome at dinner. There
is something so intimate and homelike and sweet
about the sight of a gracious host moving in and
(55) out of the room, not banging doors and disap-
pearing to another part of the house, to leave you
lonesome and skeptical until return, but just step-
ping out of vision for a mere moment, able to
keep up the conversation, and back almost be-
(60) fore you notice your companion is gone. And all
the while the food is being set upon the shining
board, and you, albeit a visitor, feel as if you were
a participant in the preparations, even as you
fondly hope to be an accessory to the deed of
(65) consumption.

Never was the kitchenette so touchingly utili-
tarian as now, when a professional chef is about
the rarest thing in modern civilization. It is the
way out for the cook of the house, his or her Dec-
(70) laration of Independence. No longer need one
fear the tyranny of the ruler of the kitchen—a
phrase fraught with ominous meanings to all
who have learned its full implications. With the
kitchenette, one can enter into a freedom not
(75) dreamed of before. One can raise a family by the
kitchenette, and it will enjoy life more than it ever
did in the kitchen days of old. No more haggard
haggling over wages or haughty laying down of
rules. The cook can now say, with one eye on the
(80) kitchenette and the other on the smiling, con-
tented faces of well-fed homebodies, "Very well,
leave if you prefer; I can get along fine without
your help."

21. The passage can be best described as which of the
following?
(A) An attempt to prove the utility of kitchenettes
(B) A whimsical argument in favor of
kitchenettes
(C) A comparison between full-sized kitchens
and kitchenettes
(D) A listing of modern time-saving devices in
domestic life
(E) An impassioned argument for the liberation
of those who cook

22. By claiming that a kitchenette will save 3 miles of
walking a day, the author intends to
(A) use hyperbole for comic effect.
(B) quantify the benefits of kitchenettes.
(C) show how modern inventions simplify our
lives.
(D) exaggerate the size of ordinary kitchens.
(E) praise the amount of work typical cooks
perform.

23. In asserting that kitchenettes improve people's
lifestyles, the author
(A) says that breakfast is the most important
meal of the day.
(B) cites how comfortable one feels as a visitor
in kitchenette homes.
(C) claims cooks will no longer want help in the
kitchen.
(D) outlines how kitchenette users save money.
(E) compares people with kitchenettes to
royalty.

24. The tone of the passage can best be described as
(A) defensive.
(B) melodramatic.
(C) progressive.
(D) pompous.
(E) austere.

25. The author emphasizes that breakfast
    - (A) is not the only meal that is ably prepared in a kitchenette.
    - (B) is the most appropriate meal for a kitchenette.
    - (C) has menu options that tend to make people hungry.
    - (D) uses each part of the kitchenette to a roughly equal degree.
    - (E) demonstrates the superior utility of the kitchenette.

26. The passage implies that hosts with full-sized kitchens tend to
    - (A) sanctify the homely details of daily living.
    - (B) neglect their guests.
    - (C) prepare meals that are far too elaborate.
    - (D) move graciously in and out of view.
    - (E) burden their guests with food preparation.

27. The passage uses the word "consumption" in line 65 to mean
    - (A) cleaning up.
    - (B) thanking a host with proper dignity.
    - (C) wasting away of the body.
    - (D) eating.
    - (E) tuberculosis.

Directions: *For questions 28–38, circle the lettered choice most nearly opposite in meaning to the word given in CAPITAL letters.*

---

28. TRANSIENT:
    - (A) municipal
    - (B) premature
    - (C) perpetual
    - (D) prescient
    - (E) intransigent

29. OBSTINATE:
    - (A) obstreperous
    - (B) pertinacious
    - (C) headstrong
    - (D) fortunate
    - (E) pliable

30. JUDICIOUS:
    - (A) imprudent
    - (B) prejudiced
    - (C) jaundiced
    - (D) entrapped
    - (E) officious

31. FOIBLE:
    - (A) infirmity
    - (B) heathen
    - (C) hypocrite
    - (D) virtue
    - (E) idiosyncrasy

32. INVIOLATE:
    - (A) inundated
    - (B) fragmented
    - (C) ventilated
    - (D) invalidated
    - (E) indoctrinated

33. EXTENUATE:
    - (A) extricate
    - (B) annihilate
    - (C) buttress
    - (D) alleviate
    - (E) enervate

34. PRISTINE:
    - (A) primordial
    - (B) sullied
    - (C) antebellum
    - (D) antithetical
    - (E) prodigious

35. SENESCENCE:
    (A) adolescence
    (B) candescence
    (C) obsolescence
    (D) acquiescence
    (E) incandescence

36. TREPIDANT:
    (A) tremulous
    (B) incisive
    (C) lateral
    (D) dauntless
    (E) languorous

37. OSTENSIBLE:
    (A) indiscernible
    (B) specious
    (C) egregious
    (D) indigenous
    (E) reprehensible

38. MARTINET:
    (A) dilettante
    (B) teetotaler
    (C) laggard
    (D) contrary
    (E) disciplinarian

Quick Answer Guide

Test 2, Part 2: Verbal (1)

1. C	11. D	21. B	31. D
2. A	12. D	22. A	32. B
3. B	13. A	23. E	33. C
4. C	14. E	24. B	34. B
5. E	15. E	25. A	35. A
6. D	16. A	26. B	36. D
7. A	17. E	27. D	37. A
8. C	18. C	28. C	38. C
9. E	19. D	29. E	
10. E	20. C	30. A	

For explanations to these questions, see Day 25.

Day 25

Test 2, Part 1: Math (1), and Part 2: Verbal (1).

Explanations and Strategies

Assignment for Today:

Review the explanations for the Math Test that you took on Day 23 and for the Verbal Test that you took on Day 24.

PART 1: MATH

1.   The correct answer is (C).

We can simplify the ratio by cross-multiplying:

$$\frac{12x}{5} = \frac{3}{y}$$

$$12xy = 15$$

Dividing both sides of the equation above by 3 yields

$$4xy = 5$$

Thus, we see that Column A equals Column B.

2.   The correct answer is (B).

We want to know which side of the triangle is larger, $\overline{MN}$ or $\overline{NL}$. To solve, we look at the angles opposite these sides. The side that has the larger angle opposite it will be longer. First, let's see what angle L is. We know that

$$(m\angle M) + (m\angle L) + (m\angle N) = 180$$

So, $46 + (m\angle L) + 89 = 180$

Or, $m\angle L = 180 - 46 - 89$

Then, $m\angle L = 45°$

We see that angle M is larger than angle L. So, $\overline{NL}$ (opposite angle M) will be greater than $\overline{MN}$ (opposite angle L). So, Column B is larger.

3.   The correct answer is (C).

Notice that $x = y$. We can determine this by the following steps:

$$x^5 - y^5 = 0$$

$$x^5 = y^5$$

And, if we take the fifth root on both sides, we get:

$$x = y$$

Therefore, for Column A, we have:

$$\frac{x^2}{y^4} = \frac{x^2}{x^4} = \frac{1}{x^2}$$

For Column B, we have:

$$\frac{1}{xy} = \frac{1}{xx} = \frac{1}{x^2}$$

So, Column A and Column B are equal.

4.   The correct answer is (C).

We can compute the quantity in Column A by following the pattern of the $\langle u \,|\, v \,|\, w \rangle$ operation:

143

$$\langle u|v|w \rangle = \frac{u}{v} + \frac{v}{w} \longrightarrow \langle 4|-2|-1 \rangle = \frac{4}{-2} + \frac{-2}{-1}$$

This problem could be tricky because of the mixture of positive and negative numbers. To get the right answer, it's important for us to deal with the signs correctly. A positive number divided (or multiplied) by a negative number is negative, so $\frac{4}{-2} = -2$, and a negative number divided (or multiplied) by a negative number is positive, so $\frac{-2}{-1} = 2$.

So $\langle 4|-2|-1 \rangle = -2 + 2 = 0$, and the two quantities are equal.

5. The correct answer is (A).

We're told that y is less than 4 but equal to or greater than –7.

Let's try Column A. We're looking for the greatest value of $-8y$. For a quantity to be "greatest," we'd like it to be positive. For $-8y$ to be positive, we'd like y to be negative so that the product of two negatives give a positive value. The greatest possible value of $-8y$ occurs when y is at its most negative value, –7. Then, the greatest possible value of $-8y$ is $-8 \times -7 = 56$.

Let's look at Column B. We want the greatest value of $14y$. Here, y should be positive so that $14y$ becomes positive. Then, the highest value y can take is just a little less than 4. It cannot take the value of 4, because we're told "$y < 4$," not "$y \leq 4$." Notice that if y were 4, $14y$ would be 56. But, because y has to be less than 4, $14y$ will always be less than 56.

So, Column A is 56 and Column B is less than 56, and the correct answer is choice (A).

6. The correct answer is (D).

There is no possible way to determine whether $\overline{KN}$ or $\overline{NL}$ is the longer segment.

7. The correct answer is (C).

We know that Clyde's bicycle wheel has a radius of 8 inches. Then, for one revolution of the wheel, Clyde's bicycle travels one circumference $= 2\pi r = 2\pi \times 8 = 16\pi$ inches. In 1 minute, the wheel turns 60 times. So, the distance traveled by the bicycle every minute is equal to 60 circumferences $= 60 \times 16\pi = 960\pi$.

Donna's bicycle has a radius of 16 inches. Then, for one revolution of the wheel, Donna's bicycle travels $2\pi r = 2\pi \times 16 = 32\pi$ inches. In one minute, Donna's wheels make 30 revolutions. So, the distance traveled by Donna's bicycle every minute is equal to 30 circumferences $= 30 \times 32\pi = 960\pi$ inches.

So, both columns are equal and the correct answer is choice (C).

8. The correct answer is (B).

The price of the sweater before December was $100. If it was marked down by 20% in December, the cost of the sweater in December was 80% of 100 = $80. The price was further reduced by half in April. So, the final price of the sweater was $40. If there was a 6% sales tax, the tax was 6% of $40 (note, it's not 6% of $100). So, the tax was $.06 \times 40 = \$2.40$, which means the total price of the sweater was 40 + 2.40 = $42.40.

Then, Column A = $42.40 and Column B = $46, which means Column B is greater than Column A.

9. The correct answer is (B).

First, let's square the expressions in the parentheses.

Then, Column A $= 7^2 \left(\dfrac{x^2}{y^2} \right) + 2^2 \left(\dfrac{x^2}{y^2} \right)$

and Column B $= 9^2 \left(\dfrac{x^2}{y^2} \right)$

Notice that $\dfrac{x^2}{y^2}$ is common to both columns. We can divide them out. Normally, this is a risky thing to do because if $\dfrac{x}{y}$ is a negative quantity, or say zero, a term that looks greater may turn out to be a greater negative, or both sides may be zero. But here we know that $\dfrac{x^2}{y^2}$ is a positive quantity.

So, if we divide the $\dfrac{x^2}{y^2}$ terms from each column, we're left with $7^2 + 2^2$ in Column A and 9^2 in Column B.

Then, Column A = 49 + 4 = 53 and Column B = 81. So, Column B is greater than Column A.

10. The correct answer is (C).

Let's list all possible values of g and h. We know that g is an even integer between 16 and 20 inclusive.

So, g can be 16, 18, or 20.

We also know that h is an odd integer between 5 and 15 inclusive.

So, h can be 5, 7, 9, 11, 13, or 15.

Finally, we know that g is twice h. Let's go down the list of possible g's:

If $g = 16$, $h = 8$ (not possible, because h should be odd).

If $g = 18$, $h = 9$ (possible).

If $g = 20$, $h = 10$ (not possible).

So, $g = 18$ and $h = 9$.

Column A = $g + h$ = 18 + 9 = 27. Column B = 27. The two are equal, and so the correct answer is choice (C).

11. The correct answer is (A).

Let's plug in values for k. k has to be a negative integer, so let's try -1. Then, Column A equals $\frac{1}{-1-1} = -\frac{1}{2}$. And, Column B is equal to $-\frac{1}{1} = -1$. In this case, Column A is greater. Now, let's see what happens when $k = -2$. Then, Column A = $\frac{1}{-32-8} = -\frac{1}{40}$ and Column B becomes $-\frac{1}{32}$. Again, Column A is greater.

For all negative values of k, the denominator (the number at the bottom) of Column A will be smaller than the denominator of Column B. This means that Column A will be more than Column B.

12. The correct answer is (D).

We can tell that the quantity in Column A is -1 times the quantity in Column B, but we don't know exactly what either quantity is. The quantity in Column A could be positive, in which case Column B would be negative and Column A would be greater. Or, Column A could be negative, in which case Column B would be positive and Column B would be greater.

Also, Column A could be zero, in which case Column B would be zero and the two quantities

would be equal. Without further information, we cannot determine which column is greater.

13. The correct answer is (B).

We can rewrite column A as: $q^2 + q^4 + q^6 = q \times (q + q^3 + q^5)$. Now look at both columns. We have:

Column A: $q \times (q + q^3 + q^5)$ and Column B: $q + q^3 + q^5$.

Now imagine dividing the entire term $(q + q^3 + q^5)$ from both columns so that we're left with q in Column A and 1 in Column B.

Note: Sometimes, it's risky to divide unknowns from both sides, especially if the unknowns can be negative numbers or zeros. But here, we're told that q is $\frac{8}{9}$, which means we can divide freely.

If we substitute the value of q, we're comparing $\frac{8}{9}$ in Column A with 1 in Column B. So, Column B is greater than Column A.

14. The correct answer is (B).

Column A is the average of three consecutive odd integers. But, the average of three consecutive odd integers is always the middle integer. For example, if the three integers are 1, 3, and 5, their sum is 9, and their average is $9 \div 3 = 3$.

So, we need to compare the middle integer (Column A) with 9 (Column B). Let's suppose that this middle integer *is* 9. Then, the smallest of the three integers must be 7 and the largest must be 11. So, the three consecutive odd integers are 7, 9, and 11.

Then, their product is $7 \times 9 \times 11 = 63 \times 11 = 693$. And their sum is $7 + 9 + 11 = 27$. The product, 693, is supposed to be 15 times the sum. Is this true? 15 times 27 is 405, not 693. Actually, 693 is about 30 times 27 (because $30 \times 20 = 600$). This tells us that 9 cannot be the middle integer.

If we choose 11 as the middle integer, watch what happens. The three integers must be 9, 11, and 13, which means their sum is 33 and their product is $9 \times 11 \times 13 = 1,287$. And now the product is close to 40 times the sum (because 30×40 is 1,200). As you can see, when we choose larger integers, the product gets larger and larger. So, we should choose smaller integers.

We found that the product was too high when 9 was the middle integer. What happens if 7 is the middle integer? Then the three integers are 5, 7, and 9. Their sum is 21 and their product is $5 \times 7 \times 9 = 315$. Is 315 equal to 15 times 21? Yes, $15 \times 21 = 315$.

So, the middle integer, which is also the average of the three integers, is 7.

In other words, Column A is 7 and Column B is 9, and so the right answer is choice (B).

15. The correct answer is (A).

Since the "6 – 2" in Column A is inside one set of << >> operators, let's subtract first, before applying the << >> rule. Then, the quantity in Column A is <<4>>. Since 4 is greater than 3, we apply the first rule:

$$<<4>> = \frac{4}{2} + \frac{1}{2} = \frac{5}{2}$$

To find the value of the quantity in Column B, let's apply the << >> rule to each number:
6 is more than 3, so we apply the first rule:

$$<<6>> = \frac{6}{2} + \frac{1}{2} = \frac{7}{2}$$

2 is less than 3, so we apply the second rule:
$$<<2>> = 2 + 1 = 3$$

So, $<<6>> - <<2>> = \frac{7}{2} - 3 = \frac{1}{2}$

We're left with $\frac{5}{2}$ in Column A and $\frac{1}{2}$ in Column B, and so Column A is greater.

16. The correct answer is (A). 5

Let's first find the value of y. We are given:
$$10,105 + y = 12,125$$
Then, $y = 12,125 - 10,105$
Or, $y = 2,020$

Now, let's find the value of $-5y$. Let's multiply both sides of the equation by -5.
Then $-5y = 2,020 \times (-5)$
Or, $-5y = -10,100$

Now, let's add 10,105 to both sides of the equation. Then, we get:
$$-5y + 10,105 = -10,100 + 10,105$$
Or, $-5y + 10,105 = 5$, which is choice (A).

17. The correct answer is (B). (u)(v)(w)(x)

We are told that the four terms $u, v, w,$ and x are odd integers between 5 and 11 and that $u < v < w < x$. Then, the values for the four terms are: $u = 5$, $v = 7$, $w = 9$, and $x = 11$. Now, let's look at the choices.

Choice (A), you will notice, is the average of the four numbers, which is the number in the middle between 5 and 11, which is 8. It is an even number. Choice (B) is the product of $5 \times 7 \times 9 \times 11$. Before you actually do the multiplying for all four terms, take two at a time: 5×7 is 35 and 9×11 is 99. Now if you multiply 35×99, you will notice that the last term of the product will end in a 5 (because the 5 of 35 times the 9 of 99 will end in a 5). So the product will be an odd number. This has to be the answer.

18. The correct answer is (D). 60,606

To find the surface area of a cube, we have to find the area of one surface and then multiply it by 6. So, the area of one surface of the smallest cube is $1 \times 1 = 1$. Then, its total surface area $= 1 \times 6 = 6$.

Speed note: At this point, you can tell that the right answer cannot be choices (B) and (E). You know why? Because the right answer has to end in a "6." You'll soon see why.

The area of one surface of the mid-sized cube $= 10 \times 10 = 100$. Then, its total surface area $= 100 \times 6 = 600$. So far, the sum of the surface areas of the two cubes is: $6 + 600 = 606$. Now check your answers. Only one answer ends in a "606," choice (D). So, you know that choice (D) has to be the right answer. But let's keep going.

The area of one surface of the largest cube $= 100 \times 100 = 10,000$. So, its total surface area $= 10,000 \times 6 = 60,000$.

So, total surface area of three cubes $= 60,000 + 606 = 60,606$, choice (D).

19. The correct answer is (B). $\sqrt{98}$

To solve this problem, we first need to find the length of $\overline{NL}$. To do this, we simply calculate the distance between the two points along the y-axis. This distance is, from N, 5 down to the x-axis plus 2 more to L. So $NL = 7$.

Now we need to find the length of *LM*. To do this, we simply calculate the distance between the two points along the *x*-axis. From *L*, it is 4 to the *y*-axis and then 3 more to *M*. So, *LM* = 7.

Notice that points *M*, *N*, and *L* form a right triangle with $\overline{MN}$ as the hypotenuse. Then,

(length of *MN*)^2 = (7)^2 + (7)^2

(length of *MN*)^2 = 98

length of *MN* = $\sqrt{98}$

20. The correct answer is (D). $0.4 \times 10^8 \pi$

We're told that the diameter is 1.28×10^4 meters. Then, the radius is half this amount, which is 0.64×10^4. (Notice that when we take half of 1.28×10^4, we take half only of 1.28. We don't take half of 10^4.)

The area of a circle is πr^2. So let's plug in the value of the radius.

Then, Area = $\pi (0.64 \times 10^4)^2$

$= \pi \times 0.64^2 \times (10^4)^2$

$= \pi \times 0.4 \times 10^8$ (because 0.64^2 is about 0.4)

$= 0.4 \times 10^8 \, \pi$.

21. The correct answer is (D). 119

Under the heading "Post-High School Plans," we see that 85 male students and 34 female students are undecided. Thus, a total of 119 students are undecided.

22. The correct answer is (D). 114

Under the heading "Sports Participation," we see that 5 percent of female students and 20 percent of male students participate in swimming. Also, we know that there are 404 female students and 468 male students.

So, the number of female students who participate in swimming is 5% of 404. Note that 10% would've been 40.4, which means that 5% is half of that, or approximately 20.

The number of male students who participate in swimming is 20% of 468. Ten percent of 468 is 46.8, which means that 20% is twice that amount, or about 93 male students.

So the total number of swimmers, both male and female, is 20 + 93, which is 113. The closest answer is choice (D), 114.

23. The correct answer is (C). 72

Under the heading "Ethnicity," we see that 59 male students and 44 female students are Hispanic. Therefore, 103 students are Hispanic.

Under the heading "Sports Participation," we see that 20% of the males and 20% of the females participate in track & field. There are 468 males, which means that the number of males who participate in track & field is

20% of 468 = $.20 \times 468 \approx 94$

Similarly, there are 404 females, which means that the number of females who participate in track & field is

20% of 404 = $.20 \times 404 \approx 81$

Then, in total, the number of students participating in track & field is: 81 + 94 = 175. Of these, we know that 103 are Hispanic students (because the problem says that all Hispanic students participate). This means that the number of non-Hispanic students participating in track & field is

175 − 103 = 72.

24. The correct answer is (C). Between 2 and 3

To answer this question, we first need to find the total number of awards won by female students. Then, we divide this number by the total number of female students in the school to get our answer.

From the heading "Number of Awards Won," we see that 58 females won 4 awards each, 154 won 3 awards each, 122 won 2 awards each, 68 won 1 award each, and 4 did not win any. So, the total number of awards won is

$58 \times 4 = 232$

$154 \times 3 = 462$

$22 \times 2 = 244$

$68 \times 1 = 68$

$0 \times 1 = 0$

Total $= 1,006$

We know that there are 404 female students. So the average number of awards won by female students is:

$$\text{Average number} = \frac{\text{Total Awards}}{\text{No. of females}}$$

$$= \frac{1,006}{404}$$

Notice that this is approximately 1,000 divided by about 400. The answer is going to be slightly more than 2, but less than 3, which means the best answer is choice (C).

25. The correct answer is (B). II only

Let's take the first option. The percent of male students who are undecided about their post-high school plans is 85 out of a total of 468. Notice that 10% of 468 would've been 46.8 and 20% would've been about 94. So, 85 is slightly less than 20%. In other words, the percent of male students who are undecided is slightly less than 20%.

There are 83 work-bound female students out of a total of 404 female students. Notice that 10% of 404 is 40.4, which means that 20% is 80.8. This means that 83 is slightly greater than 20%.

So, for the first option, the percent of male students who are undecided is less than 20% and the percent of female students who are work-bound is greater than 20%. Clearly, the first option is false. At this point, we can knock out choices (A), (D), and (E) because they all contain option I. We're now left only with choices (B) and (C).

Let's look at the second option. We know that there are 872 students in Jefferson High. Half of this (50%) is 436, and the number of male students is 468. This means that more than 50% of the students are males, and so the second option is true. Now we know that the right answer has to have option II in it. From the remaining choices, we can knock out choice (C), and we're left with only choice (B). Notice that, by eliminating the incorrect answer choices, we didn't even have to look at the third option.

26. The correct answer is (A). 17

In problems dealing with averages, it's easier to work with sums. The sum of the numbers is always equal to the average times however many numbers there are. For example, if the average of three numbers is 6, their sum is $6 \times 3 = 18$.

In this problem, the sum of 12 numbers = 276.

If four numbers are removed, there are eight numbers.

The average of these eight numbers = 26.

So, the sum of the eight numbers = $26 \times 8 = 208$

Then, the sum of the numbers removed = $276 - 208 = 68$

So, if the sum of the 4 numbers removed is 68, their average = $68 \div 4 = 17$.

27. The correct answer is (D). 92

There are five tick marks between 0 and 50, and so each tick mark is 10 units long. Point B is four tick marks from P. So, $PB = 40$.

We know that AB is 30% more than PB. In other words, AB is 130% of PB (because 30% *more* means we should add 30% to 100%).

If $PB = 40$, then $AB = 1.3 \times PB$.

(Note: AB is *not* $0.3 \times PB$.)

So, $AB = 1.3 \times 40 = 52$.

If $AB = 52$, then PA, which gives us the value of A, is $52 + 40 = 92$.

28. The correct answer is (C). 7:00 p.m.

The first train travels 40 miles every hour, and the distance it has to travel is 480 miles. So, to get to station B, it will take $480 \div 40 = 12$ hours. So, if it leaves the station A at 11 a.m., it will arrive at station B at 11:00 p.m.

The second train travels 120 miles every hour. So, it will take $480 \div 120 =$ four hours to get to station B. If it has to get to station B by 11:00 p.m. (the time that the first train gets there), it should leave four hours before 11:00 p.m., or at 7:00 p.m.

29. The correct answer is (C). 5:2

We have three important unknowns in this problem: the distance between town W and town X (let's call it a), the distance between town X and town Y (let's call it b), and the distance between Y and Z (and let's call this distance c). It may be helpful to us to draw a diagram:

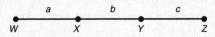

The question asks for the ratio of the distance from X to Y to the distance from Y to Z, or $b{:}c$.

Note that we don't know how far it is from any town to any other town—whether it's one mile or 100 miles or a million miles—and it doesn't matter. What's important in this problem is the relative distances between the towns. Let's assume that the total distance from W to Z is 1. One mile? One carrot? It doesn't matter.

Then the average segment is $\frac{1}{3}$. The distance from W to X is $\frac{1}{4}$ larger than $\frac{1}{3}$, so we write $a = \frac{1}{3} + \left(\frac{1}{3} \times \frac{1}{4}\right) = \frac{5}{12}$. The distance between W and Y, that is $a + b$, is $\frac{5}{6}$, so we know $b = \frac{5}{6} - \frac{5}{12} = \frac{5}{12}$. Finally, since we know that a, b, and c must add up to 1, $c = 1 - \frac{5}{12} - \frac{5}{12} = \frac{2}{12}$. And so $b{:}c = \frac{5}{12} : \frac{2}{12}$, or 5:2.

30. The correct answer is (C). 6

This looks like a very difficult problem. It is—if we don't start from the answers. If we plug in choices, it's not too bad. Let's start from the answers. Because we're looking for the *most* number of games, let's start from the highest end, choice (D), 7.

If the player played in seven games and his overall average was three goals per game, the total number of goals he scored must be $7 \times 3 = 21$. Let's see if this works.

In the first two games, the player scored two goals, which means in the next five games, he must have scored $21 - 2 = 19$ goals. Does this give us an average of *at least* four goals per game? No. Because if the average over five games was *at least* four goals, the total number of goals should be at least 20. Choice (D) doesn't work. Zap it.

Let's try choice (C), 6. If he played in six games, and his overall average was three goals per game, the total number of goals he scored must be $3 \times 6 = 18$. We know he scored two goals in the first two games. So, in the next four games, he must have scored $18 - 2 = 16$ goals. Does this give us an average of *at least* four goals? Yes, because $16 \div 4 = 4$. This works, and so choice (C) is the right answer.

PART 2: VERBAL

1. The correct answer is (C). lucrative

Use clues from the sentence to anticipate what kind of word best fits in the blank. Because Olivia's company grew rapidly, you would expect it to make a lot of money. A word like "profitable" will likely be the correct answer. Choice (C) fits just right: Her company became *lucrative*, which is to say, profitable.

Because the cyberware industry was just beginning to boom, Olivia's small technology company grew rapidly and quickly became *lucrative*.

2. The correct answer is (A). retiring..handsome

Notice that this sentence gives you two words that describe Brian in reality: *unattractive* and _____. Then you have two words that describe Brian over the phone: _____ and *outgoing*. The flag words "even though" signal that these pairs should contrast with each other. And they do. Choice (A) gives you the logical pairing: Brian changes from *unattractive* to *handsome* and from *retiring* to *outgoing*. *Retiring* means shy.

Even though Brian was unattractive and *retiring*, whenever he talked on the phone, he acted as though he were the most *handsome* and outgoing man in the world.

3. The correct answer is (B). placate..discontented

Using clues in the sentence, you should be able to see that the first blank needs a word that means something like "please" or "satisfy," while the second blank should have a word that means something like "cranky." Choice (B) fits best. To *placate* means to satisfy. *Discontented* means unhappy.

The newborn's incessant wailing convinced the young mother that it was impossible to *placate* her *discontented* infant.

4. The correct answer is (C). deciphered

The meaning of the Egyptian hieroglyphics is *still* ("remains") a mystery to us, long after something happened. What could have occurred for them to *keep* being a mystery? Perhaps the best strategy is to read in each choice to see which one works. Choice (C), *deciphered*, means decoded: The hieroglyphics are still a mystery even after they've been decoded. So, we know what the pictures represent, but we still don't know their meaning. This sentence makes sense.

The meaning of the original Egyptian "picture writing" remains a mystery to modern civilizations long after these ancient hieroglyphics have been *deciphered*.

5. The correct answer is (E). atelier..assiduously

This sentence provides plenty of clues to let you know which words will work in the blanks. The artist has a habit of working hard every night in some workspace. Of all the choices, (E) works best. An *atelier* is an artist's workroom. *Assiduously* means diligently. These words make the best sense.

Every night, the artist would lock herself in her *atelier* and work *assiduously* to finish all her paintings in time for her exhibition.

6. The correct answer is (D). seminal

This sentence is giving us a definition and asking us to supply the missing word. A foundational essay is a *seminal* essay; *seminal* means original and influential.

7. The correct answer is (A). anodyne..idyllic

The flag word "while" indicates that the two missing words are opposite to the words "shocking" and "disturbing." All the choices describe what people may think about advertisements, but only one choice contrasts with "shocking" and "disturbing."

Anodyne refers to something that relieves pain or distress. And *idyllic* means ideal, soothing. So, while many think that ads sell ideas and commodities by presenting pleasurable, attractive, and soothing images, some ads try to shock or disturb in order to reach their audience. Even if you don't know the meaning of *anodyne* and *idyllic*, if you noticed the flag word "while," you could still eliminate those choices that are not opposite to "shocking" and "disturbing."

While many think of advertisements as being uniformly *anodyne* and *idyllic*, some of the most shocking and disturbing pictures in the media may be found in ads.

8. The correct answer is (C). moisture:precipitation

smoke—a substance that comes from fire.
conflagration—fire.
  Smoke is a sign of *conflagration*.
  Is *moisture* a sign of *precipitation*? Yes. Therefore, *smoke* is to *conflagration* as *moisture* is to *precipitation*.

9. The correct answer is (E). jacket:warmth

bulwark—a barrier that obstructs passage.
privacy—a quality of being alone.
  A *bulwark* provides *privacy*.
  Is a *jacket* something that provides *warmth*? Yes.

10. The correct answer is (E). sincerity:guile

gravity—a dignity or sobriety of bearing, seriousness.
mirth—hilarity, laughter, glee.
  Gravity is the absence of *mirth*.
  Is *sincerity* the absence of *guile*? Yes. *Sincerity* describes activity that is honest. *Guile* has to do with trickery and dishonesty.

11. The correct answer is (D). bombastic:demure

garrulous—to be excessively talkative.
laconic—to be extremely terse and concise.
  Garrulous is the opposite of *laconic*.
  Is *bombastic* the opposite of *demure*? Yes. To be *bombastic* is to be showy or pompous, while to be *demure* is to be shy and timid.

12. The correct answer is (D). malice:animosity

flattery—insincere or excessive praise.
sycophancy—self-seeking, obsequious flattery.
  Flattery is a sign of *sycophancy*.
  Is *malice* a sign of *animosity*? Yes. *Malice* means ill will, and *animosity* means hatred.

13. The correct answer is (A). war:treaty

car—a vehicle moving on wheels.
brake—something used to slow down or stop movement.
  Brake is a device for slowing down or stopping the motion of a *car*.
  A *treaty* is a device (an agreement made by negotiation) that helps slow down and/or stop a war in progress, just as a brake helps slow down or stop a car in motion.

14. The correct answer is (E). eclipse:surpass

parlay—to increase or otherwise transform in value.
transform—to change the composition, appearance, or structure of something.
  Parlay means to *transform*.
  Does *eclipse* mean to *surpass*? Yes.

15. The correct answer is (E). glowing:flaming

pliant—bending easily, flexible, easily influenced.
obdurate—unmoved, unyielding, or stubborn.
  Pliant is opposite in meaning to *obdurate*.
  Is *glowing* opposite in meaning to *flaming*? Yes, if you think very hard. *Glowing* implies bright light without flame. *Flaming* implies bright light with a flame.

16. The correct answer is (A). dead:corpse

tiny—extremely small.
homunculus—a person who is extremely small, a midget.
  Tiny is the defining characteristic of a *homunculus*.
  Is *dead* the defining characteristic of a *corpse*? You bet, because if something isn't *dead*, it can't be a *corpse*.

17. The correct answer is (E).

This passage does many things in a very short space. It talks a little about the history of pearls; it describes how pearls are made, both natural and artificial; and it describes how pearls are hunted and harvested. Because the passage is so short, none of the topics receives a lot of attention. This passage is simply an overview—an introduction of sorts.

18. The correct answer is (C).

At the end of paragraph three, the passage explicitly states that artificial pearls are not as large or colorful as natural pearls. You probably could have guessed this, right?

19. The correct answer is (D).

Toward the end of the third paragraph, the author gives a simple list of how to make pearls. The iron pellet idea is not mentioned. An iron pellet was used to stimulate a real oyster to make real pearls. Therefore, this step is not part of the process for making artificial pearls.

20. The correct answer is (C).

The passage specifically states that collecting pearls from the ocean is a stinky business. The irony is that from all the stench comes an object of great beauty and value. We can infer that those who wear the pearls would probably never be the ones who would be willing to harvest them from the sea.

21. The correct answer is (B).

No matter how you look at it, the passage is an argument—it outlines the reasons why kitchenettes are so great. However, the argument is not totally serious. The author has a lot of fun in describing the virtues of kitchenettes—so much fun, we may well call it whimsical.

22. The correct answer is (A).

This line is funny, isn't it? Of course, no cook is going to walk around the kitchen for more than 3 miles each day. That's crazy. Therefore, we can conclude that the author is exaggerating (or using *hyperbole*—a gross overstatement) to be funny.

23. The correct answer is (E).

The point of paragraph three is to show how kitchenettes increase a person's standard of living. The author compares people with kitchenettes to kings and queens, saying that kitchenettes create royal luxuries, such as free time and delicious food.

24. The correct answer is (B).

The passage is humorous because it exaggerates, making a big deal out of little things. We can call this melodrama. Note how much emotion goes into describing the kinds of food kitchenette owners can eat and what kind of freedom they will enjoy. The language is unnecessarily grandiose; the author uses big, silly words when small ones would work fine. This passage is a performance of sorts.

25. The correct answer is (A).

The first part of paragraph four states that breakfast is not the only meal that can be prepared in a kitchenette. The author then describes how the kitchenette works well in other settings: for lunch, dinner, and entertaining.

26. The correct answer is (B).

The end of the fourth paragraph makes the point that people with kitchenettes can be more attentive hosts. On the other side of the coin, people with full-sized kitchens tend to spend too much time away in the kitchen, leaving their guests "lonesome and skeptical."

27. The correct answer is (D).

"Consumption" can have a wide variety of meanings, but the best meaning in this context is "eating." That's pretty straightforward, especially since the passage is all about food preparation.

28. The correct answer is (C). perpetual

Transient means short in duration.
Perpetual means going on forever. Is *perpetual* the opposite of *transient*? Yes.

29. The correct answer is (E). pliable

Obstinate means stubborn.
Pliable means yielding readily. Is *pliable* the opposite of *obstinate*? Yes, a stubborn person is not *pliable*.

30. The correct answer is (A). imprudent

Judicious means prudent, sensible.
Imprudent means unwise. Is *imprudent* the opposite of *judicious*? Yes, unwise is the opposite of sensible.

31. The correct answer is (D). virtue

Foible means defect or peculiarity.
Virtue means without defect. Is *virtue* the opposite of *foible*? Yes—without a defect is the opposite of defective.

32. The correct answer is (B). fragmented

Inviolate means unbroken, undivided.
Fragmented means broken, incomplete. Is *fragmented* the opposite of *inviolate*? Yes, these words demonstrate broken versus unbroken.

33. The correct answer is (C). buttress

Extenuate means to lessen.
Buttress means to support or strengthen. Is *buttress* the opposite of *extenuate*? Yes, to strengthen is the opposite of to lessen.

34. The correct answer is (B). sullied

Pristine means in newest state, untouched.
Sullied means spoiled, dirtied. Is *sullied* the opposite of *pristine*? Yes—it's a case of dirty versus clean.

35. The correct answer is (A). adolescence

Senescence means seniority, old age.
Adolescence means the process of growing up. Is *adolescence* the opposite of *senescence*? Yes, youth and old age are opposites.

36. The correct answer is (D). dauntless

Trepidant means timid, trembling.
Dauntless means fearless. Is *dauntless* the opposite of *trepidant*? Yes, someone fearless would not be timid.

37. The correct answer is (A). indiscernible

Ostensible means apparent.
Indiscernible means not distinct. Is *indiscernible* the opposite of *ostensible*? Yes, not distinct is the opposite of distinct or apparent.

38. The correct answer is (C). laggard

Martinet means a strict disciplinarian.
Laggard means one who procrastinates, who does not have the discipline to finish tasks. Is *laggard* the opposite of *martinet*? These are close to being opposites and the best of the five choices.

Day 26

Test 2, Parts 3A and 3B:
Issue Essay and Argument Analysis

Sample Topics

Assignment for Today:

Write an issue essay and an argument analysis on the given topics.

For the following exercise, set aside 75 minutes of uninterrupted time (45 minutes for the position paper and 30 minutes for the argument analysis), and take this test under real test-like conditions.

ISSUE ESSAY

Present your perspective on the issue below, using relevant reasons and/or examples to support your views. Time limit: 45 minutes.

"People cannot be successful through conformity and adoption of traditional practices. To get ahead, people must be willing to take risks."

ARGUMENT ANALYSIS ESSAY

Discuss how well reasoned you find this argument. Time limit: 30 minutes.

The following is a memorandum written by a manager of Indigo Books.

"Violet Books has been steadily increasing its market share. To compete with Violet Books, and to make Indigo Books profitable again, we should open an Internet café in our stores. Internet cafés tend to attract a younger population, one that spends more money purchasing books and music videos. Internet cafés would also reshape our image so that people perceive Indigo Books as being more hip than Violet Books."

Test 2, Part 4: Math (2).

Questions and Answers

Assignment for Today:

Take the second part of a practice GRE Math Test under actual test conditions. Allow yourself exactly 30 minutes to complete the 30 questions on this test.

Directions: For questions 1–15, each question contains two quantities—one on the left (Column A) and one on the right (Column B). Compare the quantities and answer

(A) if Column A is greater than Column B

(B) if Column B is greater than Column A

(C) if the two columns are equal

(D) if you cannot determine a definite relationship from the information given

Never answer (E)

In some questions, information appears centered between the two columns. Centered information concerns each of the columns for that question only. Any symbol in one column represents the same value if it appears in the other column.

	Column A	Column B

$$11 + \frac{10}{3} = \frac{4}{3} + x$$

1. | x | $15\frac{2}{3}$ |

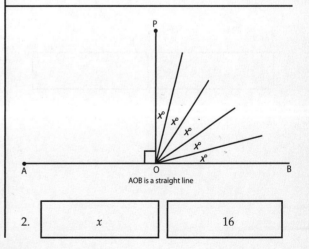

AOB is a straight line

2. | x | 16 |

Column A	Column B

3.

$(5.998)^3$	216

Stadium A seats x number of people. Stadium B seats y fewer people than Stadium A, where y is a positive number.

4.

The average (arithmetic mean) number of people that can be seated in the two stadiums	$x - \left(\frac{1}{2}\right)y$

a is an integer.

5.

7^a	$2(7)^a$

6.

a	b

Column A	Column B

S is the sum of the series $(3, 6, 9, \ldots\ldots 24)$.

T is the sum of the series $(9, 18, 27, \ldots..72)$.

7.

$\dfrac{S}{T}$	$\dfrac{1}{3}$

F = temperature in Fairbanks = –10 degrees

A = temperature in Anchorage

J = temperature in Juneau

$F > A > J$

8.

$(A)(J)$	$(AJ)^2$

9.

x	y

10.

235(63)	63(230) + 63(5)

Column A	Column B

x ounces of Type A milk contain y calories.

11. | The number of calories in c ounces of Type A milk | The number of calories in d ounces of Type A milk |

The area of a circle is 25π.

12. | The ratio of the radius to the area | $(5\pi)^{-1}$ |

$xy > 0$

13. | $\dfrac{1}{x} + \dfrac{1}{y}$ | $\dfrac{xy}{x+y}$ |

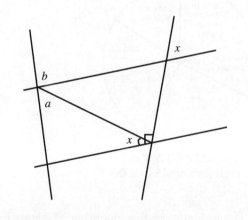

14. | $a + b$ | 90 |

Column A	Column B

A right triangle has perpendicular sides of lengths x and y and a hypotenuse of length z. Both x and y are less than 1.

15. | z^2 | $x + y$ |

Directions: For questions 16–30, solve each problem, and circle the appropriate answer choice, A–E.

16. What is the value of $10\pi + \dfrac{10\pi}{2} + \dfrac{10\pi}{200} + \dfrac{10\pi}{2000}$?
 (A) 5.055π
 (B) 5.55π
 (C) 10.055π
 (D) 15.055π
 (E) 15.55π

17. Which of the following is the largest integer smaller than $-\dfrac{7}{3}$?
 (A) −3
 (B) −2.4
 (C) −2
 (D) −1
 (E) 2

18. What is the value of $(p - q)$, if
 $r = 3$
 $s = 5$
 $p = r - s$
 $q = s - r$

 (A) −4
 (B) −10
 (C) 0
 (D) 4
 (E) 10

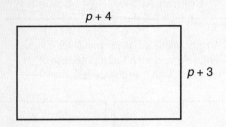

$p + 4$

$p + 3$

19. If the area of the rectangle is 42, what is a possible value of p?

(A) -3

(B) 3

(C) $\sqrt{30}$

(D) 7

(E) $17\frac{1}{2}$

20. One gallon of water can water 2 trees or 10 house plants. How many gallons are needed to water 25 house plants and 5 trees?

(A) $2\frac{1}{2}$

(B) 4

(C) 5

(D) 6

(E) 13

Questions 21–25 are based on the given figure.

1995 Earnings of Company X and Company Y, Percent by Month

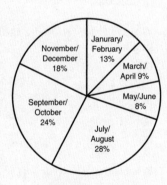

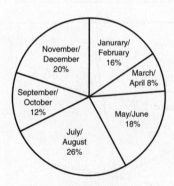

COMPANY X
Total Earnings: $300,000

COMPANY Y
Total Earnings: $400,000

21. How much more money did Company X earn during the July/August period than during the November/December period?

(A) $3,000

(B) $24,000

(C) $30,000

(D) $54,000

(E) $84,000

22. During how many two-month periods shown did Company X earn less than Company Y in the same period?

(A) 1

(B) 2

(C) 3

(D) 4

(E) 5

23. For the September/October period, Company X earned how much more than Company Y?

    (A) $14,000

    (B) $24,000

    (C) $36,000

    (D) $48,000

    (E) $72,000

24. Among the 6 two-month periods shown, the ratio of Company X's largest two-month earnings to Company Y's smallest two-month earnings is approximately

    (A) 0.23

    (B) 0.38

    (C) 2.6

    (D) 3.5

    (E) 4.3

25. In 1996, Company X's total earnings remained the same from the previous year's total earnings, but its earnings in the January/February period increased by 7% from its earnings in the same period in 1995. Company X's earnings in January/February 1996 were approximately what percent of its total earnings for 1996?

    (A) 7

    (B) 14

    (C) 17

    (D) 20

    (E) 22

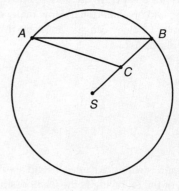

26. In the figure above, S is the center of the circle and arc AB is one quarter of the circle's circumference. If the radius of the circle is 6, and BC is one half of the radius, what is the area of $\triangle ABC$?

    (A) 6

    (B) 9

    (C) $\dfrac{9}{2}\sqrt{5}$

    (D) 18

    (E) 9π

27. A company distributes 10 percent of its profits to its shareholders and invests the rest. If the total amount invested by the company as a result of profits was $100, what was the company's profit in dollars?

    (A) $\dfrac{100}{9}$

    (B) 90

    (C) $\dfrac{1000}{9}$

    (D) 110

    (E) 190

28. A child has one penny, one nickel, one dime, one quarter, and one half-dollar. How many different amounts of money can she make by using only *two* of her coins?

    (A) 5

    (B) 10

    (C) 15

    (D) 20

    (E) 25

29. If w, r, and t are positive integers and $w + r + t = 16$, which of the following is the *least* possible value of $w(r + t)$?

    (A) 0

    (B) 15

    (C) 16

    (D) 28

    (E) 39

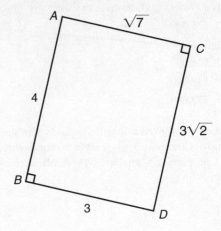

30. What is the area of the quadrilateral *ABCD*?

    (A) $3\sqrt{14}$

    (B) $6 + \dfrac{3}{2}\sqrt{14}$

    (C) 12

    (D) $18\sqrt{14}$

    (E) $12 + 3\sqrt{14}$

Quick Answer Guide

Test 2, Part 4: Math (2)

1. B	9. A	17. A	25. B
2. A	10. C	18. A	26. B
3. B	11. D	19. B	27. C
4. C	12. C	20. C	28. B
5. B	13. D	21. C	29. B
6. A	14. C	22. E	30. B
7. C	15. B	23. B	
8. B	16. D	24. C	

For explanations to these questions, see Day 28.

Day 28

Test 2, Parts 3A and 3B: Issue and Argument Responses; Part 4: Math (2), Explanations and Strategies

Assignment for Today:

Analyze your issue essay and argument analysis from Day 26 and review the Math Test you took on Day 27.

ISSUE ESSAY

The issue essay asked you to present your perspective on the following passage:

> "People cannot be successful through conformity and adoption of traditional practices. To get ahead, people must be willing to take risks."

In this section, instead of writing another passage, we would like to present you with some points that you could use to write your paper. First, following the strategy we have been adopting in this book, you should determine whether you will support the argument, oppose it, present a qualified support of it, or question the assumptions. Then, you should make a list of points that you will argue. First, fill out the following diagram:

<u>Your position</u> (underline one or more):

Support	Oppose	Qualified support	Question assumption

Then, write down the points that you will make.

1. _____

2. _____

3. _____

4. _____

5. _____

<u>Your position</u> (underline one or more):

Support   <u>Oppose</u>   Qualified support   <u>Question assumption</u>

Here are some points that you might make:

- This passage makes a sweeping generalization. By not qualifying "people," we are left with the assumption that the stated claim applies to *all* people. You can challenge this claim by talking about some people (e.g., your friends, family members) who have achieved success by conforming.

- Argue that what is meant by "conforming" is not defined. By whose standards? Would we all agree that a particular behavior is a sign of conformity? Or is it a sign of "adapting" to real-life situations?

- Argue that what is meant by "success" is not defined. One person might define success as earning a million dollars. Another might define it as being happy. Similarly, you could argue that an individual's success (e.g., inventing a product) could be a familial failure (the inventor's children considered their parent to be neglectful of them in the pursuit of invention).

- Argue that what is meant by "traditional practices" is not defined. One person's tradition (e.g., not attending college) may be another's sign of rebellion.

- Draw a distinction between "willing to take risks," which seems to be the passage's gold standard for success, and "actually taking risks," which, you could argue, is more meaningful.

- You might point out that, if everyone defied traditional practices of thinking, it would lead to anarchy and lawlessness.

- Remember that, in the issue essay, you can also *support* the given premise. So, you could say that, under some conditions, the passage is correct. You could then give examples from history of people who defied conventional wisdom and went on to achieve success.

- You can also express a qualified agreement with the passage. Hence, you might say that there are examples of both types of successful people: those who defied and those who followed traditional practices.

ARGUMENT ANALYSIS

The passage for the argument analysis was:

> "Violet Books has been steadily increasing its market share. To compete with Violet Books, and to make Indigo Books profitable again, we should open an Internet café in our stores. Internet cafés tend to attract a younger population, one that spends more money purchasing books and music videos. Internet cafés would also reshape our image so that people perceive Indigo Books as being more hip than Violet Books."

Before writing the passage, if you followed the strategy we proposed, you wrote down a list of assumptions and/or conclusions that you would address. If you did not, do so now. Then, see the next page for some ideas you might have used in your essay.

Assumption 1: _____

Assumption 2: _____

Assumption 3: _____

Assumption 4: _____

Assumption 5: _____

Conclusion 1: _____

Conclusion 2: _____

Instead of writing an essay, we provide you here with some "talking points" with which to construct your arguments.

- An Internet café might promote more browsing but fewer sales of books.
- A café would need additional staff members.
- A café may incur additional expense to get suitable building/restaurant permits.
- Indigo Books may have a reputation as a bookstore without any "frills," and the addition of a café might be construed as selling out to the latest trend.

- We know that Violet Books has been increasing its market share, but we don't know whether the market served by Violet Books is the same as the one served by Indigo Books.
- Maybe other steps (e.g., having a computerized database) can improve Indigo's profits.
- Does having a hip image lead to more profits?
- Would patrons to the café spend most of the time on computers and not spend time buying books?

PART 4: MATH

1.   The correct answer is (B).

The equation is $11 + \dfrac{10}{3} = \dfrac{4}{3} + x$

Subtract $\dfrac{4}{3}$: $11 + \dfrac{10}{3} - \dfrac{4}{3} = x$

$11 + \dfrac{6}{3} = x$

$11 + 2 = x$

$x = 13$

So, Column A = 13 and Column B = $15\dfrac{2}{3}$, which means Column B is greater than Column A.

2.   The correct answer is (A).

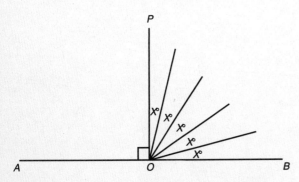

In the figure, $\angle AOP$ = 90 degrees, which means that $\angle POB$ is also 90 degrees (because $\angle AOB$ is a straight line). This 90-degree angle is divided into 5 equal angles, each x degrees. So, the measure of each of these small angles is $90 \div 5 = 18$ degrees.

Hence, Column A is greater than Column B.

3.   The correct answer is (B).

Don't even attempt to find the third power of 5.998. There's something else going on here. 5.998 is a little smaller than 6 and $6^3 = 216$, so 5.998^3 must be less than 216.

4.   The correct answer is (C).

Instead of working with x and y, let's plug in our own values. Just to make things simple, let's say that

$x = 10$ and $y = 2$ (this is a pretty pathetic stadium if it seats only 10 people, right? But who cares!)

So, Stadium A can seat 10 people, and Stadium B can seat $10 - 2 = 8$ people. The average then is $\dfrac{(10+8)}{2} = 9$. So, Column A = 9.

Column B = $x - \left(\dfrac{1}{2}\right)y = 10 - \left(\dfrac{1}{2}\right)2 =$ $10 - 1 = 9$.

So, Column A = Column B.

5.   The correct answer is (B).

Let's see what happens if a is 1.

Then,   Column A = $7^1 = 7$

And   Column B = $2(7)^1 = 14$.

Here, Column B is greater. Or, if $a = 0$,

Then,   Column A = $7^0 = 1$

And   Column B is $2(7)^0 = 2 \times 1 = 2$.

(Don't forget that any number raised to a power of 0 is equal to 1.)

And, what happens if a is a negative number, say, –1?

Then,   Column A = $7^{-1} = \dfrac{1}{7}$

And   Column B = $2(7)^{-1} = \dfrac{2}{7}$.

Notice that, because 7 is a positive number, 7^a will always be a positive number, too, and Column B will always be twice as large as Column A. Hence, the right answer is choice (B).

6.   The correct answer is (A).

We see that the two sides of the given triangle are equal to x. This means that the triangle is an isosceles triangle. In an isosceles triangle, the two angles opposite, or facing, the equal-length sides are equal. In other words, angles $5a$ and $6b$ are equal. So, we can write: $5a = 6b$.

Dividing both sides of the equation by 5, we get

$a = \dfrac{6}{5}b$

In other words, a is greater than b (because a is actually 1.2 times b), and the right answer is choice (A).

7. The correct answer is (C).

Notice that the second series is identical to the first series, except that every term in it is 3 times the corresponding term in the first series. In other words, the first term, 9, is 3 times the first term, 3. The second term, 18, is 3 times the second term, 6, and so on, up to the last term.

This tells us that the sum of all numbers, T, in the first series is going to be 3 times the sum of all numbers, S, in the second series. In other words, we can write the following equation:

$T = 3S$

Dividing both sides by T, we get:

$$1 = \frac{3S}{T}$$

Dividing by 3, we get:

$$\frac{1}{3} = \frac{S}{T}$$

In other words, Column A is equal to Column B.

8. The correct answer is (B).

Let's suppose that the temperature in Anchorage, A, is 1 degree lower than the temperature in Fairbanks. Then, $A = -11$.

Also, let's assume, just to make things simple, that the temperature in Juneau, J, is 1 degree lower than the temperature in Anchorage. So, $J = -12$.

Then, Column A $= (A)(J) = (-11)(-12)$. Notice that this will be a positive number (because a negative times a negative is positive).

And, Column B $= (AJ)^2 = (-11)(-12) \times (-11)(-12)$. So, we can set up the comparison as follows:

Column A $= (-11)(-12)$

Column B $= (-11)(-12) \times (-11)(-12)$

We can divide out the common terms $(-11)(-12)$ from both sides, and we're left with 1 in Column A and $(-11)(-12)$ in Column B. Notice that Column B is positive and much larger than 1, which means Column B is greater than Column A.

9. The correct answer is (A).

The key here is to know that, in a triangle, the largest side is always opposite the largest angle, the smallest side is always opposite the smallest angle, and so on.

In the given figure, y is opposite angle $2p$, and x is opposite the largest angle, $6p$. So, x is the largest side, which means x is greater than y.

10. The correct answer is (C).

Let's look at Column A, 235(63). What if we break 235 down into 230 + 5? Then we get (230 + 5)63. Now if we multiply each term within the parentheses by 63, we get (230)63 + (5)63, which is exactly what we see in Column B, so the two columns are equal.

11. The correct answer is (D).

Just to make things easier, let's suppose that x is 1 and y is 1. Then, we know that 1 ounce of milk contains 1 calorie.

Column A: How many calories in c ounces?
c calories.

Column B: How many calories in d ounces?
d calories.

Now, which is greater? We have no way of knowing. What if c were 1 and d were 10 million? Then, Column B would be greater. And, if c were 1 and d were 1, the two columns would be equal. So, without knowing the relationship between c and d, we have no way of knowing which column is greater.

12. The correct answer is (C).

We know that the area of a circle is: $A = \pi r^2$, where r is the radius. We're given that the area of the circle is 25π. Then we can write:

$$25\pi = \pi r^2$$

Or,

$$25 = r^2$$

This means that the radius of the circle, r, is 5. Now, Column A wants us to find the ratio of the radius to the area. This is

$$\frac{radius}{area} = \frac{5}{25\pi} = \frac{1}{5\pi}$$

But, another way of writing $\frac{1}{5\pi}$ is $(5\pi)^{-1}$.

So, the two columns are equal.

13. The correct answer is (D).

To solve this problem, let's plug in our own numbers. We know that $xy > 0$. This simply means that neither x nor y is zero. So, what happens if $x = 1$ and $y = 10$, just for fun?

Then, Column A $= \frac{1}{x} + \frac{1}{y} = \frac{1}{1} + \frac{1}{10} = 1 + .1 = 1.1$,

And Column B $= \frac{xy}{x+y} + \frac{1 \times 10}{1+10} = \frac{10}{11}$

This means that Column A is greater than Column B. Now what happens if, say, $x = -1$ and $y = -10$ (notice that xy is still greater than 0).

Then, Column A $= \frac{1}{x} + \frac{1}{y} = \frac{1}{-1} + \frac{1}{-10} = -1 + (-.1) = -1.1$

And Column B $= \frac{xy}{x+y} + \frac{(-1)(-10)}{(-1)+(-10)} = \frac{10}{-11} = -\frac{10}{11}$

So, here Column A is negative 1.1, and Column B is negative $\frac{10}{11}$. Notice that $\frac{10}{11}$ is less than 1.1, which means that $-\frac{10}{11}$ is actually more than –1.1. So, in this example, Column B is actually greater than Column A.

As soon as we get two different results, we know that the right answer has to be choice (D).

14. The correct answer is (C).

First, let's mark the given diagram, as shown here.

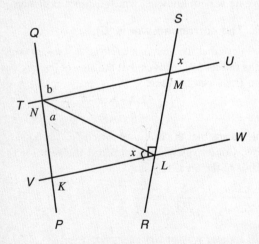

We know that m∠SMU = m∠NML (they are called vertical angles, and vertical angles have equal measure). This means that m∠NML is also x. Notice that

m∠KLM is given to be 90 degrees and m∠KLN is x. So, then, m∠NLM must be $90 - x$.

Then, in triangle NLM, one angle is x, another is $90 - x$, and the third angle is ∠MNL. We know that the three angles in a triangle must sum to 180 degrees.

So, $\quad x + (90 - x) + \text{m}\angle MNL = 180$

$$90 + \text{m}\angle MNL = 180$$

$$\text{m}\angle MNL = 90$$

Now look at the straight line QNP. We know that $a + \text{m}\angle MNL + b = 180$. But, m∠MNL = 90. So we have: $\quad a + 90 + b = 180$.

Or $\qquad\qquad\qquad a + b = 90$.

In other words, Column A is equal to Column B.

15. The correct answer is (B).

From the geometry of a right triangle, we know that $z^2 = x^2 + y^2$.

Since x and y are both less than 1, $x^2 < x$ and $y^2 < y$. (If you don't see why this is so, consider what would happen if $x = .5$. Then, $x^2 = .25$, which is less than x.) Thus, $z^2 = x^2 + y^2 < x + y$.

Or, another way to solve this problem is to plug in values for x and y. Suppose $x = .5$ and $y = .5$. Then, $x^2 = y^2 = .25$. And, we know that $z^2 = x^2 + y^2 = .25 + .25 = .5$. Further, $x + y = .5 + .5 = 1$. So, $z^2 = .25$ and $x + y = 1$.

16. The correct answer is (D). 15.055π

Let's scan the answers. All choices are in terms of π. So, there's no need to convert π to its numerical value.

The first two terms of the problem, $10\pi + \frac{10\pi}{2}$, tell us that the answer has to be more than 15π because $\frac{10\pi}{2}$ equals 5π and $10\pi + 5\pi = 15\pi$. Zap choices (A), (B), and (C).

Now, let's look at the third term, $\frac{10\pi}{200}$. This equals $\frac{\pi}{20}$, which is $.05\pi$ because $\frac{1}{20} = .05$. When we add this term to 15π, we get 15.05π. At this point, we know the answer has to be choice (D), because choice (E) is too high. The addition of the last term $\frac{10\pi}{2000}$ is much too small for choice (E) to be correct. (Because the last term, $\frac{\pi}{200}$ is only $.005\pi$.)

17. The correct answer is (A). –3

In order to solve this problem, it's necessary to know that integers include negative numbers, zero, and positive numbers (without a fractional component). The number $-\frac{7}{3}$ can be simplified to $-2\frac{1}{3}$. We need the next smaller integer, which means we want the quantity to be "more negative."

In other words, we want a bigger whole number with a negative sign. The next number that is less than $-2\frac{1}{3}$ is –3, which is choice (A). Note that the correct answer is not –2 or –1 because these numbers are greater than $-2\frac{1}{3}$.

18. The correct answer is (A). –4

Let's plug in values of r and s in the given equations. We're told that $r = 3$ and $s = 5$.

Then,

$$p = r - s = 3 - 5 = -2$$

$$q = s - r = 5 - 3 = 2$$

Then $p - q = -2 - 2 = -4$, which is choice (A).

19. The correct answer is (B). 3

We are given that the area of the rectangle, which is the product of the length and width, is 42. Then, we can write

$$(p + 4)(p + 3) = 42$$

To get the answer, we can expand the two parentheses in the equation and solve for p. (Yeah, right!) We have a better way, don't we? We plug in values from the answer choices.

We could start with choice (C)—if we were Einstein. We don't want to get anywhere close to that choice. Let's start with choice (D) and plug in the value of 7 for p.

Then, $(7 + 4)(7 + 3) = 42$

Or $11 \times 10 = 42.$

No, it doesn't work. And we see that the value of p is too high. At this point, we can zap choices (D) and (E). Let's go backward and try choice (B), 3 (notice, we're still avoiding the ugly radical sign; hey, that's not illegal). Plugging in the value of 3, we get $(3 + 4)$ $(3 + 3) = 42$

Or, $7 \times 6 = 42.$

It works, and so choice (B) is the right answer.

20. The correct answer is (C). 5

Let's break this down into trees and plants and take them separately.
Trees: One gallon waters 2 trees. So, for 5 trees, we'll need

$$\frac{5}{2} = 2\frac{1}{2} \text{ gallons.}$$

Plants: One gallon waters 10 plants. So, for 25 plants, we'll need

$$\frac{25}{10} = 2\frac{1}{2} \text{ gallons.}$$

So, the total amount of water needed is

$$2\frac{1}{2} + 2\frac{1}{2} = 5 \text{ gallons.}$$

21. The correct answer is (C). $30,000

From the given chart, we see that Company X earned 28% in July/August and 18% in November/December. So, the earnings in July/August exceeded the earnings in November/December by 28% – 18% = 10%.

We know that $300,000 is the total earnings. So, 10% of this amount is $.10 \times 300,000 = \$30,000$.

22. The correct answer is (E). 5

January/February: Without calculating the actual amount, we can tell that Company X earned less than Company Y (because the percent amount is less and the total earnings are less for Company X than for Company Y).
March/April: For Company X, 9% of $300,000 is $27,000, and for Company Y, 8% of $400,000 is $32,000. So, this period also counts toward our answer.
May/June: Again, without calculating the actual amount, we can see that Company X earned less than Company Y (because the percent amount is less and the total earnings are less for Company X than for Company Y). This period also counts.
July/August: Company X's earnings are 28% of $300,000 = $84,000, and Company Y's earnings are 26% of $400,000 = $104,000. This period should also be counted. (So far, we have four periods; let's keep going.)
September/October: Company X's earnings are 24% of $300,000 = $72,000, and Company Y's earnings are 12% of $400,000 = $48,000. So, this period does not count.

November/December: Company X's earnings are 18% of $300,000 = $54,000, and Company Y's earnings are 20% of $400,000 = $80,000. This period also counts.

Hence, we see that, of the 6 two-month periods, only the September/October period does not count. In other words there are 5 two-month periods when Company X's earnings were less than Company Y's earnings for the same period.

23. The correct answer is (B). $24,000

First, we want to find the amount earned by Company X during the September/October period. Then, we want to find the amount earned by Company Y during the same period. From this, we can determine how much more Company X earned than Company Y.

During September/October, Company X earned 24% of $300,000, which is .24 × 300,000 = $72,000.

In the same period, Company Y earned 12% of $400,000, which is .12 × 400,000 = $48,000.

So, Company X's earnings exceeded Company Y's earnings by $72,000 – $48,000 = $24,000.

24. The correct answer is (C). 2.6

Company X's largest earnings occurred during the July/August period, which was 28%. The dollar amount is 28% of $300,000 = .28 × 300,000 = $84,000. Company Y's smallest earnings occurred during the March/April period, which was 8%. So, the dollar amount is 8% of $400,000 = .08 × 400,000 = $32,000. Then the required ratio is $\frac{84,000}{32,000} = \frac{84}{32} = \frac{21}{8}$, which is greater than 2 and slightly less than 3. In other words, our answer should be greater than 2 but less than 3. We can see that choice (C), 2.6, is the closest.

25. The correct answer is (B). 14

In 1995, Company X's earnings during the January/February period were 13%. In dollars, this is .13 × 300,000 = $39,000. We know that, in the following year, earnings during the same period increased by 7%. So, to find the dollar amount, let's first find 7% of $39,000. It is

.07 × 39,000 = $2,730.

So, the earnings for January/February 1996 are $39,000 + $2,730 = $41,730. We can approximate this to $42,000.

We know that the total earnings did not change in 1996. In other words, Company X's total earnings were still $300,000.

Now we need to know what percent of $300,000 is $42,000. This is given by the ratio

$$\frac{42,000}{300,000} \times 100 = \frac{42}{300} \times 100 = \frac{42}{3} = 14$$

So the correct answer is 14%.

26. The correct answer is (B). 9

We're told that arc AB is one quarter of the circumference. This means that m∠ASB is 90 degrees (because 90 degrees is one quarter of the total number of degrees in a circle, which is 360). So, let's draw this 90-degree angle by connecting A and S.

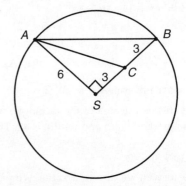

Then, AS is also 6 because it's another radius. We're told that BC is half the radius. In other words, BC = SC = 3. We need to find the area of triangle ABC. We can take $\overline{BC}$ to be the base. We now need the height. To find the height, we need a 90-degree angle from the base to the opposite corner of the triangle.

If we extend $\overline{BC}$ to S, we see that the height of the triangle = AS = 6. Remember, height is simply a perpendicular line from the base to the opposite corner. It's not necessary for $\overline{SC}$ to be part of the triangle. So now we know the height and the base. Then, the area is

$$A = \frac{1}{2}bh,$$

So, $A = \frac{1}{2} \times 3 \times 6 = 9$

27. The correct answer is (C). $\frac{1000}{9}$

Let's work from the answers and plug values back into the problem. As usual, we start with choice (C), $\frac{1000}{9}$. This is supposed to be the company's profit.

Well, if this is the profit, then we know that 90% of this amount should equal $100. Why? Because we're told that 10% is given back to the shareholders and the rest (which is 90%) is invested. We're also told that the total amount invested is $100.

In other words, 90% of $\frac{1000}{9}$ should be equal to 100.

That is, $.90 \times \frac{1000}{9} = 100.$

Or, $\frac{90}{100} \times \frac{1000}{9} = 100.$

This equation is true, so choice (C) is the answer. Notice how easy it was once we started from the answers. Always look for this shortcut.

28. The correct answer is (B). 10

Each of the five coins can combine with the four others. So, $5 \times 4 = 20$ combinations.

penny + nickel	PENNY COMBINATIONS
penny + dime	
penny + quarter	
penny + half-dollar	
nickel + penny	NICKEL COMBINATIONS
nickel + dime	
nickel + quarter	
nickel + half-dollar	
dime + penny	DIME COMBINATIONS
dime + nickel	
dime + quarter	
dime + half-dollar	
quarter + penny	QUARTER COMBINATIONS
quarter + nickel	
quarter + dime	
quarter + half-dollar	
half-dollar + penny	HALF-DOLLAR COMBINATIONS
half-dollar + nickel	
half-dollar + dime	
half-dollar + quarter	

But notice that each of the combinations is counted twice in this operation. (For example, *penny + half-dollar* is the same amount as *half-dollar + penny*; both equal 51 cents!) So, half of these combinations are repeats! So, half of 20 = 10 *different* amounts.

29. The correct answer is (B). 15

We are looking for the *least* possible value of $w(r + t)$. We should start from the lowest end of the answer choices, which is choice (A), 0. Is it possible for $w(r + t)$ to be 0 if w, r, and t are all positive integers?

$w(r + t) = 0$ only if $w = 0$ (which is not allowed because w is a positive integer) or if $r = -t$ (which is also not allowed because both r and t have to be positive). So, choice (A), 0, is not possible.

Let's see if choice (B), 15, is possible. To get the least value for $w(r + t)$, we should let w be the smallest of the three because it is being multiplied by both r and t. Choose w to be the smallest positive integer, 1.

Then, if $w = 1$, $r + t$ has to equal 15 so that $w + r + t = 16$. Now, $w(r + t) = 1(15) = 15$. This is the answer.

30. The correct answer is (B). $6 + \frac{3}{2}\sqrt{14}$

We cannot simply multiply the length and the width of the quadrilateral because it's not a rectangle (although it looks like one). It has two different lengths and two different widths. But notice that we're given two right angles. Yes, we can construct two right triangles if we draw a diagonal from B to D.

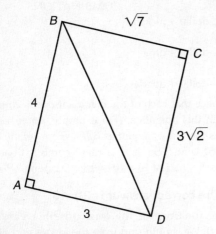

Then, the area of the right triangle *ABD* is

$$A_{\triangle ABD} = \frac{1}{2} \times AD \times AB$$

$$= \frac{1}{2} \times 3 \times 4$$

$$= 6$$

And the area of the right triangle *BCD* is

$$A_{\triangle BCD} = \frac{1}{2}bh$$

$$= \frac{1}{2}BC \times CD$$

$$= \frac{1}{2} \times \sqrt{7} \times 3\sqrt{2}$$

$$= \frac{3}{2}\sqrt{14}$$

Now, we simply add these two values together to find the entire area of *ABCD*.

$$A_{ABCD} = 6 + \frac{3}{2}\sqrt{14}$$

Test 2, Part 5: Verbal (2), Questions and Answers; Test 2, Part 6: Issue and Argument Responses

Assignment for Today:

Take the second part of a practice GRE Verbal Test and the second part of the writing assignment under actual timed conditions. Allow yourself 30 minutes to complete the 38 questions in the test and 75 minutes for the two writing assignments (45 minutes for the issue essay and 30 minutes for the argument analysis).

VERBAL TEST

Directions: *For questions 1–7, one or more words have been left out of each sentence. Circle the answer, A–E, that contains the word or words that best fit the meaning of the entire sentence.*

1. Working hard to ____ the requirements of his current position, Clarence became the next person in line for a promotion.
   (A) scorn
   (B) assert
   (C) misjudge
   (D) fulfill
   (E) amplify

2. Our city's extensive and versatile public transit network offers the nation's most ____ means of travel, from trains and cable cars to the many electric and diesel busses.
   (A) expensive
   (B) varied
   (C) questionable
   (D) exciting
   (E) private

3. When the DNA sample from the ____ murderer did not match the sample from the murder weapon, the suspect was ____ in the public's mind.
   (A) convicted..blamed
   (B) alleged..released
   (C) famous..incriminated
   (D) accused..exonerated
   (E) transient..exculpated

4. When the Andersons' infant cried all night, it severely ____ the young couple's volatile relationship; furthermore, the ____ task of caring for a new baby required more energy than the new parents had to give.

   (A) exacerbated..relentless
   (B) enhanced..simple
   (C) aggravated..pleasing
   (D) mitigated..arduous
   (E) solidified..tedious

5. Dress styles among female White House staff members have abruptly switched from Kappa Gamma Kappa to ____, including everything from long, flowing skirts and suede vests to threadbare jeans.

   (A) Neolithic
   (B) eclectic
   (C) indelicate
   (D) demure
   (E) comfortable

6. It was within the ____ of the queen to ____ her husband's unpopular decree.

   (A) domain..chastise
   (B) puissance..instigate
   (C) purview..rescind
   (D) temerity..delineate
   (E) disparagement..repeal

7. The widespread fascination with the novel is generated by the ____ of possible interpretations that resist reduction to a single voice.

   (A) plethora
   (B) anathema
   (C) quorum
   (D) enigma
   (E) regalia

Directions: For questions 8–16, determine the relationship between the two words given in capital letters. Then, from the choices listed A–E, select the one pair that has a relationship most similar to that of the capitalized pair. Circle the letter of that pair.

8. COBWEBS:DISUSE::
   (A) mirage:condensation
   (B) telephone:isolation
   (C) treaty:agreement
   (D) road:industrialization
   (E) rust:paint

9. WANE:DIMINISH::
   (A) curse:praise
   (B) recover:discover
   (C) exhort:exile
   (D) pawn:buy
   (E) inter:bury

10. CLEVER:OBTUSE::
    (A) graceful:maladroit
    (B) trite:obsequious
    (C) rustic:homely
    (D) precocious:sagacious
    (E) abstruse:universal

11. SPEECH:BLURTING::
    (A) wind:gusting
    (B) muscle:releasing
    (C) rain:misting
    (D) vision:sparkling
    (E) hearing:amplifying

12. SOLILOQUY:MONOLOGUE::
    (A) tire:car
    (B) script:play
    (C) solo:duo
    (D) human:mammal
    (E) silence:noise

13. REGALE:AMUSEMENT::

  (A) marry:engagement

  (B) relish:delight

  (C) endorse:approval

  (D) rule:authority

  (E) renege:agreement

14. POIGNANT:BANAL::

  (A) wet:frigid

  (B) frozen:thawed

  (C) fatuous:trite

  (D) moldy:mildewed

  (E) eternal:forever

15. DIPLOMAT:CONCILIATORY::

  (A) demagogue:unemotional

  (B) iconoclast:unconventional

  (C) seer:uninspired

  (D) dogmatist:unassertive

  (E) pundit:uninformed

16. ABROGATE:VOID::

  (A) debilitate:healthy

  (B) derogate:admired

  (C) endorse:valid

  (D) encumber:possible

  (E) endanger:protected

Directions: *For questions 17–27, read each passage and answer the questions that follow. Base your answers only on what is stated or implied in the passage.*

Questions 17–20 are based on the following passage.

France at the end of the Fifteenth Century had fully recovered from the effects of the English wars. The devastated fields were again culti-vated; civilization had returned to the districts
(5) from which foreign invasion and civil war had banished it. Observers speak of the country as flourishing throughout its length and breadth; the population was increasing, and commerce showed an unprecedented volume and activity.
(10) The great towns, large and self-governed, were centers of industrial life, and were the chief pro-vincial capitals. Probably no country in Europe possessed such inherent power for resistance or attack. England had hardly yet recovered from
(15) the War of the Roses, and the Tudors did not feel themselves quite secure upon the throne. Italy was richer and more civilized, but so disunited as to be helpless. Neither the Empire nor Spain possessed such a strong or popular monarchy as
(20) France.

The European world generally was passing through a very critical stage in its perpetual transformation. Vast changes in the very consti-tution of European society had come in the last
(25) two centuries; the materials for further unsus-pected revolutions in politics and religion were accumulated on every side. The medieval con-ception of things was almost dead, and though the institutions that had been generated by that
(30) conception still presented an imposing appear-ance, they were seriously threatened—all the more seriously because they did not suspect the coming attack. The shock which the Church had received by the so-called Babylonian Captivity,
(35) the Great Schism, and the Great Councils of the Fifteenth Century had shaken the very founda-tions of its power, both secular and spiritual, though the external traces of the blows had been very nearly smoothed away. The mind of Europe,
(40) no longer satisfied with the old ideas, was feel-ing after new ideas and new guides and was developing new and unsuspected energies.

Printing had come on the heels of the New Learning. Columbus had found land beyond the
(45) Atlantic waters, and this and other geographical discoveries gave an incalculable impetus to people's thoughts and imaginations. However, it was not only the explorers who were ready to push away from the old landmarks into un-
(50) known waters. Italy was the first country that was affected by these new ideas, which soon passed from Italy to France and were eagerly welcomed there. The effects were far-reaching.

17. The major purpose of this passage is to

   (A) describe the rejuvenation of Europe after the demise of religious institutions.

   (B) recognize the role France played in being the primary source of ideas that transformed post-fifteenth-century Europe.

   (C) demonstrate how technological discoveries such as printing and Columbus' geographical discoveries provoked the imagination.

   (D) analyze the impact of a popular monarchy upon a country's overall dynamic or static tendencies.

   (E) describe the conditions that made France a fertile environment for accepting revolutionary thought.

18. The author uses Columbus' discovery of land beyond the Atlantic as an example of

   (A) a technological breakthrough born of the ferment in newly stirred imaginations.

   (B) how people were willing to explore unknown waters and go abroad.

   (C) a changing reality that inspired people to break the bonds of parochial thought.

   (D) an historical event that had immeasurable impact on modern civilizations.

   (E) the superior ability of European nations to extend their geographical boundaries.

19. The passage implies that

   (A) dissatisfaction with the monarchy prevented people in most European nations from being receptive to new ideas.

   (B) France flourished because its population increased during post-war peace and harmony.

   (C) France's quick recovery from the English wars had its roots in agricultural rebirth.

   (D) most medieval institutions were weakened by their failure to recognize the changing climate of thought and ideas.

   (E) France eagerly welcomed new ideas because they originated in Italy.

20. The critical stage in the transformation of fifteenth-century Europe was characterized by all of the following EXCEPT

   (A) stability in the belief of traditional concepts and values.

   (B) a general dissatisfaction with old ideas in the minds of most European countries.

   (C) institutions conceived in medieval times being undermined.

   (D) an accumulation of new thoughts and ideas in politics and religion.

   (E) weakening of the Church's power in matters both secular and spiritual.

Questions 21–27 are based on the following passage.

   A diligent searcher along any beach or coastline will be sure sometimes to light upon curious and valuable specimens, especially after violent storms may such be sought for with the greatest
(5) chance of success, for the agitation of the waters will then have loosened them from their natural beds and dwelling places and cast them on the shore. Very frequently, however, they will be so beaten about and defaced that they will be com-
(10) paratively valueless; if enveloped in tangled masses of seaweed, they are likely to be preserved from injury, and such heaps of uprooted marine vegetation will often afford a rich harvest to the young conchologist, who should always
(15) carefully examine them. Many of the shells are so minute as scarcely to be seen with the naked eye; therefore, this search can scarcely be properly effected without the assistance of a pocket lens, the cost of which is but trifling. The under-
(20) sides of pieces of stranded timber, the bottoms of boats lately returned from a fishing voyage, the fisherman's dredge or net, the cable, and the deep-sea line; all these may prove productive, and should be looked to whenever opportunity
(25) offers. Nor should the search for land and fresh-water shells be neglected, for many of these are very curious, as well as beautiful, and no conchological collection is complete without them. For these, the best hunting grounds are the
(30) ditch-side and the riverbed, the mossy bank and the hedgerow, amid the twining, serpentine roots

of the old thorn and elder trees, the crevices of the garden wall, the undersides of stones, and all sorts of out-of-the-way holes, nooks, and corners,
(35) where may be found the Striped Zebra, and other prettily marked snail shells, and many other kinds worthy of a place in a collection.

When live shells—those that have the living fish in them—are obtained, the best plan is to
(40) place them in spirits or wine. This at once deprives the inhabitants of life, without injuring the shell, which should then be placed in hot water for a time. The body of the mollusk is thus rendered firm, and may be removed by means
(45) of some pointed instrument. Care should be taken to leave no portion of animal matter within, or after a while it will become putrid and give out a stain, which will show through and injure the delicate markings of the shell. The sur-
(50) est, most expeditious, and least troublesome mode of cleansing a shell is to place it in an ant heap for a day or two; the busy little insects will penetrate into its inmost cavities, and remove hence all offending matter. There will be no dif-
(55) ficulty in this respect with the multivalve and bivalve kinds, which are only kept closed by means of a set of muscles which can be tightened or relaxed at the pleasure of the animal within, and become powerless to keep the shell closed
(60) as soon as that is dead. Great care must be taken to preserve unbroken the smaller parts of these shells, such as the hinges or teeth. The beard, also, as it is called, and silky threads, must not be removed, as these have much to do in deter-
(65) mining the particular species.

River and land shells are generally very thin and brittle, and must be carefully handled. Their colors are not usually so brilliant as those of the marine species, but they form links in the
(70) testaceous chain, which are necessary to a proper study and elucidation of conchology.

The most glowing and gorgeous of all shells are those brought from the tropical seas, and, excepting a few rare instances, specimens of most
(75) of these can be obtained at little cost from any dealer, or from friends returning from a voyage.

If it is necessary to send those any distance, or to pack them away, the best plan is to wrap them separately in soft paper, place them in a box,
(80) and then pour in sawdust, bran, or fine sand, very dry, until all the open spaces are completely filled up.

21. The primary purpose of the passage is to
    (A) demonstrate that seashell collecting can be interesting and rewarding.
    (B) explain the primary difference between ocean shells and river shells.
    (C) instruct shell collectors on the basic means of finding, preparing, and transporting shells.
    (D) describe the best kinds of seashells to have in a collection.
    (E) motivate readers to begin shell collecting as a hobby.

22. Who is the primary audience for this passage?
    (A) Professional conchologists
    (B) Budding conchologists
    (C) Recreational beachcombers
    (D) Travelers
    (E) Novices

23. With which of the following statements would the author most likely DISAGREE?
    (A) A good time to collect shells is after storms.
    (B) Shells were once houses for sea animals.
    (C) A good collection should have all types of shells.
    (D) A good conchologist will handle shells carefully.
    (E) Sometimes collectors forget to search for land shells.

24. With which of the following statements would the author most likely DISAGREE?

   (A) Nature exists for our enjoyment and use.

   (B) Readers will have access to natural environments.

   (C) Conchology is a worthwhile pursuit.

   (D) Preserving sea life is more important than preserving shells.

   (E) Sea shells can be injured.

25. In comparing ocean shells with river shells, the author of the passage implies that

   (A) river shells are more valuable.

   (B) ocean shells are more brittle.

   (C) river shells are less beautiful.

   (D) river shells should have a higher priority in a collection.

   (E) river shells are more dangerous to collect.

26. The passage states that the problem with leaving animal matter inside a shell that is part of a collection is that

   (A) the value of the shell decreases.

   (B) the shell will discolor.

   (C) ants will invade the collection.

   (D) animals deserve to be set free.

   (E) the shell will soon break.

27. In paragraph two, the author advises the reader to leave the beard and teeth of a shell intact because

   (A) they show that shells have features like humans.

   (B) they injure the delicate markings of the shell.

   (C) they can be used to extract the body of the mollusk.

   (D) they attract ants that help clean the shell.

   (E) they help identify the species.

Directions: *For questions 28–38, circle the lettered choice most nearly opposite in meaning to the word given in CAPITAL letters.*

28. LACONIC:

   (A) pithy

   (B) verbose

   (C) ostensible

   (D) disorganized

   (E) holographic

29. ACUTE:

   (A) homely

   (B) attractive

   (C) obtuse

   (D) jocund

   (E) discredited

30. TRIBUTE:

   (A) panegyric

   (B) cenotaph

   (C) entropy

   (D) sodality

   (E) censure

31. TANTAMOUNT:

   (A) salubrious

   (B) identical

   (C) paramount

   (D) contradistinctive

   (E) incomparable

32. APROPOS:

   (A) inapposite

   (B) germane

   (C) de rigueur

   (D) ludic

   (E) manic

33. SEDITION:
    (A) credulity
    (B) fealty
    (C) treason
    (D) erosion
    (E) derision

34. VEX:
    (A) abrade
    (B) hex
    (C) mollify
    (D) jinx
    (E) modulate

35. PERSPICACIOUS:
    (A) injudicious
    (B) prescient
    (C) orotund
    (D) juridical
    (E) sagacious

36. COETANEOUS:
    (A) subcutaneous
    (B) execrative
    (C) phlegmatic
    (D) primeval
    (E) contemporary

37. PROTEAN:
    (A) impuissant
    (B) antediluvian
    (C) antidromic
    (D) mutable
    (E) abiding

38. ELUTRIATE:
    (A) extricate
    (B) vitiate
    (C) adulterate
    (D) objurgate
    (E) ensorcell

Quick Answer Guide

Test 2, Part 5: Verbal (2)

1. D	11. A	21. C	31. D
2. B	12. D	22. B	32. A
3. D	13. C	23. C	33. B
4. A	14. B	24. D	34. C
5. B	15. B	25. C	35. A
6. C	16. C	26. B	36. D
7. A	17. E	27. E	37. E
8. C	18. C	28. B	38. C
9. E	19. D	29. C	
10. A	20. A	30. E	

For explanations to these questions, see Day 30.

ISSUE ESSAY

Present your perspective on the issue below, using relevant reasons and/or examples to support your views. Time limit: 45 minutes.

> "Organizations should strive to use technology that increases efficiency so that people have more free time."

ARGUMENT ANALYSIS ESSAY

Discuss how well reasoned you find this argument. Time limit: 30 minutes.

The following appeared in a memorandum from the provost of The Technology College:

> "Our competition, Harris Community College, has increased its long-distance student base by 40% over the last five years, and its operating costs have decreased dramatically. During the same period, The Technology College saw a sharp drop in student enrollment and our maintenance costs have increased, leading to a $3 million budget deficit. To become more competitive and to improve our financial situation, we should promote Internet-based programs in our college."

ISSUE ESSAY SAMPLE RESPONSE

The issue essay asked you to comment on the following passage:

> "Organizations should strive to use technology that increases efficiency so that people have more free time."

Following the strategy we have been adopting in this book, you should determine whether you will support the argument, oppose it, present a qualified support for it, or question the assumptions. Then, you should make a list of points that you will argue. First, fill out the following:

<u>Your position</u> (underline one or more):

Support	Oppose	Qualified support	Question assumption

Then, write down the points that you will make.

1. _____

2. _____

3. _____

4. _____

5. _____

Here is a sample position with some points you might make.

<u>Your position</u> (underline one or more)

Support   <u>Oppose</u>   Qualified support   <u>Question assumption</u>

- The passage rests on the assumption that having more free time is a good thing. You could challenge this in a number of ways:
  - Some people may currently have too much free time.
  - Having more free time may introduce temptations into people's lives—things (e.g., gambling) that people have no time to do when they're very busy.
  - Having more free time may make us lazier.

- The idea that being more efficient will result in more free time rests on the assumption that time saved by being more efficient will be used toward being more "free." But this saved time may be used to do more work!

- The passage rests on the assumption that having more or less free time is a function of technology. It may be a function of how we think and what we value.

- The passage assumes that everyone in the organization has access to or likes to use technology.

- Over time, our technologies have certainly allowed us to become more efficient (e.g., we can now send instant e-mail), but do we have more leisure time today than we did in the past?

- Finally, the passage also rests on the assumption that how a technology will be used can be controlled.

ARGUMENT ANALYSIS SAMPLE RESPONSE

The passage for the argument analysis was:

"Our competition, Harris Community College, has increased its long-distance student base by 40% over the last five years, and its operating costs have decreased dramatically. During the same period, The Technology College saw a sharp drop in student enrollment and our maintenance costs have increased, leading to a $3 million budget deficit. To become more competitive and to improve our financial situation, we should promote Internet-based programs in our college."

Before writing the essay, if you followed the strategy we proposed, you wrote down a list of assumptions and/or conclusions that you would address. If you did not, do so now. Then, see the next page for some ideas you might have used in your essay.

Assumption 1: _____

Assumption 2: _____

Assumption 3: _____

Assumption 4: _____

Assumption 5: _____

Conclusion 1: _____

Conclusion 2: _____

Here are some "talking points" with which you could construct your arguments.

- The passage assumes that The Technology College can replicate the success of Harris Community College. You can challenge this assumption. Maybe the two colleges have very different reputations.

- The two colleges may also cater to very different kinds of students. It could be that Harris has students who are professionals with day jobs (for whom telecommuting would make more sense), whereas Technology students are more conventional.

- It could be that enrollment at Technology has diminished because of its reputation, which will not be cured by installing long-distance degree programs.

- Maybe the mission of a college is not to increase profitability.

- If maintenance costs have risen at Technology, those expenditures are not likely to decrease by adding long-distance degree programs because existing buildings will have to be maintained regardless.

- Maybe having predominantly more distance-learning students will hamper the quality of on-site education because social interactions between students would suffer.

Test 2, Part 5: Verbal (2).

Explanations and Strategies: Final Review of Writing Assessment

Assignment for Today:

Review the explanations for the Verbal Test you took on Day 29 and do a final review of the writing assessment.

PART 5: VERBAL

1. The correct answer is (D). fulfill

Reading the sentence, you should understand that Clarence is a hard worker and ready to get a promotion. This means he must have followed the requirements of his current job. With this in mind, you can look for a positive word. The two positive words are *fulfill* and *amplify*. *Fulfill* sounds right; *amplify* doesn't, since it means to enlarge, to heighten, to increase. One would not increase the requirements for a job in order to get a promotion.

Working hard to *fulfill* the requirements of his current position, Clarence became the next person in line for a promotion.

2. The correct answer is (B). varied

This sentence tells us that the public transportation system in our city is "extensive and versatile," which indicates that the system is large and can do lots of different things. "Trains and cable cars. . . many electric and diesel buses" tells us that there are a lot of choices. All these elements together indicate that the

network offers various, or *varied*, means of travel. Trying each of the choices in the sentence may have helped you find the correct choice.

Our city's extensive and versatile public transit network offers the nation's most *varied* means of travel, from trains and cable cars to the many electric and diesel buses.

3. The correct answer is (D). accused..exonerated

The sentence should give you adequate clues to come up with your own words to fill in the blanks. You probably won't think of the exact words given in the choices, but you can find synonyms. The context indicates that an investigation is under way, and the murderer is merely a suspected murderer, not a convicted one. *Accused* works well. Not finding a DNA match should make the accusation less believable, so *exonerated*, which means freed from blame, works well.

When the DNA sample from the *accused* murderer did not match the sample from the murder weapon, the suspect was *exonerated* in the public's mind.

4.   The correct answer is (A). exacerbated..relentless

From the clues in the sentence, you should be able to guess the kinds of words that will adequately fill the blanks. The verb in the first blank should mean something like "made worse." *Exacerbated* is the right word here. The second blank should describe tasks of caring for a new baby. Actually, many words might work here—depending what you think of caring for babies—but the word *relentless* works with the rest of the sentence. *Relentless* means never-ending, which certainly would add stress to a marriage.

When the Anderson's infant cried all night, it severely *exacerbated* the young couple's volatile relationship; furthermore, the *relentless* task of caring for a new baby required more energy than the new parents had to give.

5.   The correct answer is (B). eclectic

This is a tough one, because the clues are located after the blank. There are no obvious flags, so perhaps the best way to work this question is to plug in choices and eliminate the ones that don't fit.

We know that the dress preference has switched to now include a wide range of clothing. And *eclectic* means "selecting or borrowing from a wide variety." If you know the definition of *eclectic*, you'll get it right. If you don't recognize the word, don't panic. See if you can eliminate at least some of the other choices.

Dress styles among female White House staff members have abruptly switched from Kappa Gamma Kappa to *eclectic*, including everything from long, flowing skirts and suede vests to threadbare jeans.

6.   The correct answer is (C). purview..rescind

The best way to find the right choice is to read the choices and eliminate those that don't make sense. The only stem pair that works together and with the logic of the sentence is choice (C). *Purview* means range of authority. To *rescind* means to make something invalid.

It was within the *purview* of the queen to *rescind* her husband's unpopular decree.

7.   The correct answer is (A). plethora

This is a vocabulary-based question. The context of the sentence tells us that we are looking for a word meaning multitude or collection: "the multitude of possible interpretations that resist reduction to a single voice." The correct choice is (A), *plethora*, which means an excess or overabundance.

These are tough words, some of which you might not have known. But had you known the meanings of some (*quorum*, for example, is the necessary number for a meeting to take place), you could have eliminated several choices and taken a better guess.

The widespread fascination with the novel is generated by the *plethora* of possible interpretations that resist reduction to a single voice.

8.   The correct answer is (C). treaty:agreement

cobweb—a web spun by a spider.
disuse—not being used.

Cobwebs are a sign of *disuse*.

Is a *treaty* a sign of *agreement*? Yes. A *treaty* is a signed document indicating that some *agreement* between parties has been reached.

9.   The correct answer is (E). inter:bury

wane—to decrease or diminish.
diminish—to decrease.

To *wane* means the same thing as to *diminish*.

Does to *inter* mean the same thing as to *bury*? Yes. Therefore, *wane* relates to *diminish* in the same way that *inter* relates to *bury*.

10. The correct answer is (A). graceful:maladroit

clever—smart and witty.
obtuse—slow, dull, and stupid.

Clever is nearly the opposite of *obtuse*.

The stem words, CLEVER:OBTUSE, should tell you that the correct choice will be a pair of opposites. Of course, you had to know that *obtuse* means dull or stupid. And the problem here is also knowing the definition of the words in the choices. Most of them were toughies.

Is *graceful* nearly the opposite of *maladroit*? You probably know what *graceful* means: pleasing or attractive in movement. But what does *maladroit* mean? *Maladroit* means lacking adroitness, or awkward. (You might have gotten a clue from the prefix, *mal-*, which means bad or poorly.) So *graceful* and *maladroit* are near opposites in the same way that *clever* and *obtuse* are near opposites.

11. The correct answer is (A). wind:gusting

speech—manner or act of speaking.
blurting—speaking suddenly.
    Blurting is when *speech* erupts suddenly.
    Is *gusting* when *wind* erupts suddenly? Yes. Therefore, *speech* is to *blurt* as *wind* is to *gust*.

12. The correct answer is (D). human:mammal

soliloquy—a speech by a person talking to himself/ herself, often used to disclose innermost thoughts.
monologue—a speech or discourse uttered by a single speaker.
    A *soliloquy* is a special kind of *monologue*.
    Is a *human* a special kind of *mammal*? Yes.

13. The correct answer is (C). endorse:approval

regale—to give amusement to, to delight.
amusement—delight, pleasure, or entertainment.
    To *regale* someone is to give them *amusement*.
    Does to *endorse* someone give them *approval*? To *endorse* a person or a project means to give one's *approval*, to support that project.

14. The correct answer is (B). frozen:thawed

poignant—extremely touching, deeply affecting the feelings.
banal—trite, common, or ordinary.
    Poignant means the opposite of *banal*.
    Does *frozen* mean the opposite of *thawed*? Yes. *Thawed* means melted.

15. The correct answer is (B). iconoclast:unconventional

diplomat—a person who makes relationships better.
conciliatory—making things more friendly, less severe.
    A *diplomat* is *conciliatory*.
    Is an *iconoclast unconventional*? Yes. An *iconoclast* is someone who fights against tradition. Therefore, *diplomat* is to *conciliatory* as *iconoclast* is to *unconventional*.

16. The correct answer is (C). endorse:valid

abrogate—to make something void.
void—without force or value.
    To *abrogate* is to make something *void*, the opposite of making something healthy or stronger.
    Is to *endorse* to make something *valid*? Yes. For example, when you endorse a check, you make it valid.

17. The correct answer is (E).

Each paragraph must contribute to the main idea. So, for each paragraph, ask, "What's your point?"
    Here, the first paragraph says, "France was flourishing like no other country." The second paragraph says, "Old European ideas were changing." The third paragraph says, "All sorts of people welcomed new, expansive ideas, especially the French."
    The three points taken together suggest that France was a flourishing, united, strong, and fertile nation where people were willing to accept new ideas and put them into practice.
    That's more or less what choice (E) says.

18. The correct answer is (C).

People had no idea there was land beyond the Atlantic. Columbus' discovery changed reality. You don't need to know that, though.
    The passage specifically states "this and other geographical discoveries gave an incalculable impetus to people's thoughts and imaginations." This means it inspired people to think beyond usual limits. That's choice (C).
    Sometimes you can locate the exact information in the passage.

19. The correct answer is (D).

The passage specifically states "the institutions. . . were seriously threatened. . .because they did not suspect the coming attack [of unsuspected revolutions in religion and politics]."

That means people were inspired to think beyond usual limits. That's choice (D).

Try to locate the exact information in the passage.

20. The correct answer is (A).

The passage specifically states that "the mind of Europe was no longer satisfied with the old ideas" and was "feeling after new ones."

21. The correct answer is (C).

This passage is written as an instructive passage for those who are at least a little interested in shell collecting. The various parts of the passage explain how to find, prepare, and transport shells.

22. The correct answer is (B).

This passage is addressed to those already interested in shell collecting, but the passage is too basic for professional conchologists—they already know this information. However, the budding conchologist would probably be eager to learn some of the tricks of the trade.

23. The correct answer is (C).

The author implies at the end of the first paragraph that certain kinds of shells are better for a shell collection. Some shells—drab shells, broken shells, common shells—the author would likely banish from a collection.

24. The correct answer is (D).

The only statement that the author would disagree with is choice (D)—preserving sea life is more important than preserving shells. In fact, the author seems not to care at all about the sea creatures who have made the shells their homes. The passage provides the reader with a quick way to dispose of the animals so the shell can be collected and preserved.

25. The correct answer is (C).

Paragraph three makes the point that river and land shells are usually less brilliant than shells from the ocean. We can safely assume that the author uses brilliance as a measure of beauty.

26. The correct answer is (B).

The middle of paragraph two says that dead animal matter left inside the shell will stain the shell. "Get those creatures out!" the author says, in so many words.

27. The correct answer is (E).

At the end of paragraph two, the author warns the reader not to remove the beard and teeth "as these have much to do in determining the particular species."

28. The correct answer is (B). verbose

Laconic means succinct, concise.
Verbose means wordy. Is *verbose* the opposite of *laconic?* Yes—*verbose* means using a lot of words whereas *laconic* means using a few well-chosen words.

29. The correct answer is (C). obtuse

Acute means sharp, severe.
Obtuse means blunt, not sharp. Is *obtuse* the opposite of *acute?* Yes, blunt is the opposite of sharp.

30. The correct answer is (E). censure

Tribute means praise.
Censure means criticism. Is *censure* the opposite of *tribute?* Yes, criticism is the opposite of praise.

31. The correct answer is (D). contradistinctive

Tantamount means same, uniform.
Contradistinctive means different by contrast. Is *contradistinctive* the opposite of *tantamount?* Yes.

32. The correct answer is (A). inapposite

Apropos means appropriate.
Inapposite means not relevant. Is *inapposite* the opposite of *apropos?* Yes.

33. The correct answer is (B). fealty

Sedition means resistance to lawful authority.
Fealty means fidelity, allegiance. Is *fealty* the opposite of *sedition*? Yes—*sedition* is lack of allegiance or *fealty*.

34. The correct answer is (C). mollify

Vex means bother.
Mollify means appease. Is *mollify* the opposite of *vex*? Yes, to appease is the opposite of to bother.

35. The correct answer is (A). injudicious

Perspicacious means shrewd.
Injudicious means unwise. Is *injudicious* the opposite of *perspicacious*? Yes, unwise is not shrewd.

36. The correct answer is (D). primeval

Coetaneous means contemporary.
Primeval means ancient, primitive. Is *primeval* the opposite of *coetaneous*? Yes, ancient is the opposite of contemporary.

37. The correct answer is (E). abiding

Protean means changeable, variable.
Abiding means unchanging. Is *abiding* the opposite of *protean*? Yes, one means not changing, the other changing.

38. The correct answer is (C). adulterate

Elutriate means to purify by washing.
Adulterate means to corrupt or make impure. Is *adulterate* the opposite of *elutriate*? Yes, it's a case of purity versus impurity.

FINAL REVIEW OF WRITING ASSESSMENT

Set aside about 90 minutes to work on the writing assessment. Designate someone you know to serve as your editor—this may be a teacher, a colleague, a family member, or a friend. Ask them to read your passages and to provide you with feedback. It will also help them if they know what to look for. We recommend that you go to the ETS Web site (www.gre.org) and download the criteria used by ETS to evaluate your passages. Provide these guidelines to your editor.

Issue Essay

Directions: *Choose one of the two topics given below, and write your position on one of them. You can accept, reject, or qualify the stated position. Make sure you provide support for the position you adopt. (Time limit: 45 minutes)*

Topic 1.

"Museums should abandon a voluntary fee structure and make their patrons pay a flat entrance fee."

Topic 2.

"The government should rate prime time television programs based on their violence and sexual content."

Argument Analysis

Directions: *Analyze the line of reasoning presented in the following passage. Note that you are not being asked to present your own views on the subject. (Time limit: 30 minutes)*

"The most dangerous vehicle on the road is the minivan. Latest statistics show that, compared to other motorized vehicles, minivans are 12 times more likely to be involved in collisions. Whereas the average collision rate, defined as the number of collisions per 1,000 vehicles, among non-minivan vehicles is 2, the average collision rate of minivans is 24. Minivan drivers should therefore be required to take extra driving lessons before they are allowed to drive on the streets. They should also be required to pay greater insurance premiums."

Issue Essay Guidelines

The first thing you need to do is decide which of the two topics you want to discuss. Note that many students spend an inordinate amount of time deciding which of the two topics they feel comfortable writing about. You should plan on spending no more than one minute in making this decision. Decide quickly and begin working on the topic.

Let's assume that you are going to write about Topic 2, rating prime-time television programs.

Prepare a short list of arguments, both for and against each side of the issue. For example, your list may look something like this:

For	Against
- reduce violence on TV	- smacks of censorship
- reduce children's exposure to violence	- reduction of creativity
	- what criteria will the government use?
	- who in the government gets to decide?
	- requires new bureaucracy
	- production time gets longer

As you can see, you have more arguments against the position than you do for the position. Note also that five or six arguments are usually sufficient to make a good case. Try not to list too many arguments because you need to demonstrate that you can write clearly and that you can think in-depth. So, let's assume that you will write against the position. Now decide the order in which you will present your arguments. It is usually a good idea to begin with your strongest argument and end with another strong argument. Perhaps the strongest argument is censorship, and so you can use it to make your first point. Reduction of creativity is perhaps the next strongest argument. You can then reorder your arguments as:

- censorship
- what criteria will the government use?
- who in the government gets to decide?
- requires new bureaucracy
- production time gets longer
- reduction of creativity

Note also that another way to develop an argument is to punch holes in the opposing side's argument. So, for example, if the opposing side would argue that we could protect children from violence on television, you might point out that this is better done by vigilant parents.

Argument Analysis Guidelines

The first thing you need to do here is to spot the conclusion that is being drawn. The two conclusions of the passage are that (a) minivan drivers should be required to take extra driving lessons and (b) their insurance premiums should be higher. This conclusion is based on a number of premises. The following chart works backward from the conclusion to the initial premise:

minivan drivers require extra lessons and higher premium ⇓

(because) minivans are more dangerous ⇓

(because) more minivans get into collisions ⇓

(because) the average collision rate is greater for minivans

Now, begin to tear down the argument. You might start from the first premise, that the average collision rate is greater for minivans. This could be true, but it's probably also true that there is nothing inherently dangerous about minivans. Rather, minivans are disproportionately more likely to have children in them, compared to other vehicles on the road. So, it could be that the disturbance to the driver (caused by children in minivans) is at the heart of collisions.

Furthermore, if disturbance, and not the vehicle type, is what causes collisions, then you might think about other sources of disturbances to the driver. These might include talking on the cell phone and eating while driving. So, if minivan drivers need to take extra lessons and pay a higher premium, then we might also require cell phone users to do the same. Or, we might make it illegal for people to eat while driving.

Finally, note that even if we were to accept the finding that minivan drivers get into more collisions, we could question the proposed solution—requiring extra driving lessons (which seems irrelevant if the problem is noisy children in the vehicle) or paying higher insurance premium (which may not be the business of government).

Overall Point

Many of the argument analysis passages make a causal claim. That is, they assert that A causes B. In this example, the cause is "type of vehicle" and the effect is "number of collisions." In order for one variable to cause another, three conditions must be met:

Condition 1: The cause must have occurred before the effect.

Condition 2: The cause and effect must "co-vary," meaning that as one occurs, the other must, too.

Condition 3: We must be able to rule out other causes for the same observed effect.

In our example, Condition 1 seems to have been met.

Condition 2 may or may not have been met. Not all minivans, after all, are involved in collisions.

Condition 3 is the most problematic. There are many other possible causes to the finding that minivans are involved in greater numbers of collisions.

Therefore, when you write the Argument Analysis, think about the three conditions noted above and see which ones can be discounted.

CONCLUSION

If you have followed this 30-Day Program, you should now be in great shape to take the GRE. By now you have taken two complete tests—12 sections in all—and you have gone over the questions and explanations. Remember that doing well on the GRE requires not only good verbal, math, and analytical skills, but also "test smarts."

In this book, you have been introduced to lots of strategies and shortcuts designed to save you time and make you test-smart. We recommend that you use whatever time you have left before your test to go back and review the test-taking, verbal, math, and analytical strategies. Then you should look over the sample tests and explanations and make sure you understand how to tackle each question type.

GOOD LUCK!